CHILD ANXIETY DISORDERS

CHILD ANXIETY DISORDERS

A Family-Based Treatment Manual
for Practitioners

JEFFREY J. WOOD
BRYCE D. M^CLEOD

Illustrations by

LAURA S. HIRUMA
AND
ANN Q. PHAN

W. W. Norton & Company
New York • London

For information about permission to reproduce
selections from this book, write to
Permissions, W. W. Norton & Company, Inc.,
500 Fifth Avenue, New York, NY 10110

For information about special discounts for bulk purchases, please contact
W. W. Norton Special Sales at specialsales@wwnorton.com or 800-233-4830.

Composition and book design by MidAtlantic Books & Journals
Manufacturing by Haddon Craftsmen
Production Manager: Leeann Graham

Library of Congress Cataloging-in-Publication Data

Wood, Jeffrey J., Ph. D.
  Child anxiety disorders : a family-based treatment manual for
  practitioners / Jeffrey J. Wood and Bryce D. M°Leod ; illustrations
  by Laura S. Hiruma and Ann Q. Phan. — 1st ed.
      p. ; cm.
  "A Norton professional book."
  Includes bibliographical references and index.
  ISBN 978-0-393-70540-9 (hardcover)
  1. Anxiety in children—Treatment. 2. Child psychotherapy—
  Parent participation. 3. Cognitive therapy for children. I. M°Leod,
  Bryce D. II. Title. [DNLM: 1. Anxiety Disorders—therapy. 2. Child.
  3. Cognitive Therapy—methods. 4. Family Therapy—methods.
  WM 172 W876c 2008]

  RJ506.A58W66 2008
  618.92'8522—dc22   2007029908

ISBN 13: 978-0-393-70540-9

W. W. Norton & Company, Inc., 500 Fifth Avenue, New York, N.Y. 10110
www.wwnorton.com
W. W. Norton & Company Ltd., Castle House, 75/76 Wells St., London W1T 3QT

9 8 7 6 5 4 3 2 1 0

This book is dedicated with love
to our parents,
James L. and Patricia A. Wood and
Donald E. and Lorita S. McLeod

Contents

• •

PART II Treatment Manual

CHAPTER 4

Building Confidence: A Family-Based Cognitive-Behavioral Intervention 71

Acknowledgments

● ●

This book began in 1999 when we became curious if we could improve upon standard cognitive-behavioral therapy (CBT) interventions for children with anxiety disorders by offering families basic communication training. Two of our faculty mentors from the UCLA Neuropsychiatric Institute, Drs. Marian Sigman and John Piacentini, were also interested in whether CBT could be augmented, and a collaboration was born. Little did we know that the "basic" family intervention we would go on to develop would become as intricate and distinct from standard CBT as it indeed became. We gratefully acknowledge Drs. Sigman and Piacentini for their mentorship, guidance, and immeasurable contributions to this program and our careers.

Although not directly involved in this project, Dr. Barbara Scales—former director of the UC Berkeley Child Study Center—had a formative influence on the concepts discussed throughout this book. Dr. Scales, a respected developmentalist and a mentor to J.J.W. since his freshman year at Berkeley, has always emphasized the value of promoting children's independence and autonomy, of ensuring that children have the opportunity to learn through hands-on experience without excessive adult direction, and of supporting children's development of close peer relationships. Each of these themes figures prominently in this book and reflects our great respect and admiration for Dr. Scales's philosophy and teachings.

Many colleagues generously volunteered to serve as therapists in the clinical trial of the treatment program presented in this book, the Building Confidence program, including Drs. Rosalie Corona, Alanna Gelbwasser, Kristin Hawley, Wei-Chin Hwang, Mandy Jensen, Erum Nadeem, and Adrienne Nishina; Drs. Michael Southam-Gerow and Brian Chu provided their CBT and family therapy expertise as supervisors during the clinical trial. Without their collective help, the trial and this book would not have been possible. Grants from the National Institute of Mental Health (F31-MH64999; R03-MH63836) were also instrumental in the development of this intervention.

J.J.W. and B.D.M.

My father, James L. Wood, had an overarching influence on the development of this book and the values underlying it. He was a professor of sociology at San Diego State University, a political activist and leader, and a well-published scholar known nationally and internationally. His values of compassion, equality, and collaboration are fundamental components of the family-based intervention described in this book. Furthermore, his mentorship throughout my life, both academically and ethically, helped make the writing of this book and the development of this intervention program possible. This book was completed near the end of my father's life and he was aware of its imminent publication. In so many ways, I could not have done it without his eternal love and support.

J.J.W.

Preface

Anxiety disorders are among the most common psychiatric problems experienced by school-age youngsters and can cause significant difficulties in their daily lives. Psychologists, school counselors, and other child mental health professionals often help children with challenging anxiety-related concerns and are in need of evidence-based therapeutic strategies. This book presents a family-focused cognitive-behavioral intervention approach, the Building Confidence program, which was developed and tested over the course of 5 years at UCLA. This program has recently been found to be more effective than standard therapy procedures for child anxiety disorders in a clinical trial sponsored by the National Institute of Mental Health (Wood, Piacentini, Southam-Gerow, Chu, & Sigman, 2006). Anxiety disorder remission rates at the posttreatment assessment were about 80%—among the highest success rates achieved in the treatment of any childhood psychological problem. This book offers step-by-step guidelines for implementing this therapeutic approach.

A key theme underlying the Building Confidence intervention is that family interaction patterns can play an important role in the development and persistence of childhood anxiety problems. Fortunately, such interaction patterns are malleable, and parents can become key allies in the treatment and alleviation of their children's anxiety. Structural and strategic family therapy concepts inform the methods and goals of the intervention. A collaborative family-based approach is used, melding potent cognitive-behavioral treatment techniques with holistic therapy practices that treat the child as a part of a system that can support his or her growth and coping. Positive and supportive family change strategies are emphasized as critical to helping the family system develop stronger, more appropriate boundaries and to enhance communication skills that can assist children in managing their anxiety.

A unique aspect of this intervention technique is that it was developed by drawing upon years of basic research on parent-child interaction patterns in families of children with anxiety disorders. This research has identified communication styles and patterns of family boundaries unique to families of children with high anxiety. Researchers have hypothesized that intervening effectively with these family processes may contribute to improvements in children's ability to cope with anxiety. The intervention presented in this book puts these concepts into practice and focuses intervention efforts specifically on the domains of family functioning most likely to influence children's experiences of anxiety.

This book is organized into two sections. In Part I, Clinical Background, foundational information is presented. Chapters begin with brief case vignettes illustrating typical features of childhood anxiety. Chapter 1 describes how anxiety manifests in school-aged children, reviews research on the natural course of childhood anxiety problems, and discusses contemporary methods for assessing anxiety in children. Chapter 2 reviews the environmental and genetic factors associated with childhood anxiety, presenting current research and theory on how children learn to fear situations and how variations in brain functioning affect children's propensity to become anxious. The role of family interactions is also taken up. In Chapter 3, evidence-based treatments for child anxiety disorders are reviewed and described. Research on this specific intervention technique is summarized, as is the rationale for the specific cognitive-behavioral and family therapy techniques that comprise the program.

In the treatment manual in Part II, session-by-session instructions for the intervention are presented. Chapter 4 provides a practical guide for clinicians to use when treating youth with anxiety disorders, including the complete treatment manual used in our clinical trial at UCLA. Practitioners working with children in a variety of settings will find the guidance provided in this section to be sufficiently detailed to inform treatment implementation with a wide range of clients. This section also provides additional details on the rationale and principles underlying each component of the intervention program in order to enhance practitioners' case conceptualization skills and flexibility in working with diverse groups of children affected by anxiety. This practical guide should ensure that professionals are well equipped to adapt the intervention program to the needs and characteristics of the populations that they serve.

PART I

Clinical Background

CHAPTER ONE

Clinical Features of Anxiety Disorders in Children

• •

"I think I'm going to lose it, mom," Spencer yelled, holding his stomach and rushing to the bathroom.

Ms. C. ran in to find her son stooped over the toilet, flushed and teary eyed. Weakly, he lowered himself to the ground and lay on his back, hands resting on his stomach. "I don't think I can go today, Mom. Please don't make me go."

Spencer has been in the fifth grade for slightly over a month and has attended a full day of school only twice. On the first day of the school year, he told his mother he did not feel up to going to school and would feel much better staying home. Ms. C. encouraged him to go and eventually was able to get him off to school. Later that day, he visited the school nurse and complained of nausea. His mother was called and she picked him up early. Subsequently, despite two medical exams suggesting that Spencer was perfectly healthy, he developed nausea and several other physical symptoms such as a racing heart, sweating, and headache each day when getting ready for school. These symptoms abated on days his mother let him stay home. As a result, although she has felt conflicted each day, she has decided not to send him or has picked him up early nearly every day.

Ms. C. looked at her son with pity and concern. "Of course, honey. You don't have to go. You're sick."

Anxiety in children can range from mild, understandable, and transient to severe, irrational, and intractable. Most children (and adults) experience some anxiety on a regular basis—so much so that it seems to be a basic part of the human experience. In fact, moderate levels of anxiety can motivate individuals to increase their level of effort and attention when working on a problem or project and thus can have a positive effect. However, high levels of anxiety can interfere with performance and negatively impact a child's ability to function at home and school (Ma, 1999; Wood, 2006a). When a child experiences high levels of anxiety consistently across time and situations, he or she may have an anxiety disorder. This chapter focuses on the nature of anxiety, the common childhood anxiety syndromes, the assessment of children's anxiety, and the negative effects that anxiety can have on children's adaptive functioning and development.

Anxiety and fear are closely related emotions and mood states that occur in response to perceptions of threat and danger (Barlow, Brown, & Craske, 1994). The focus is on negative future events that might, but will not necessarily, occur. In children and adults, anxiety is linked with unpleasant physical sensations (e.g., nausea), negative mood, and thoughts about possible negative events (e.g., failing a test, embarrassing oneself, being lost). These sensations and worries gradually dissipate once the possible danger passes, leading to a sense of relief. The concept of the fight-or-flight reflex is closely related to high levels of anxiety and fear—for instance, children often avoid situations that make them very anxious (i.e., flight).

Even though periodic experiences of anxiety and fear are common for most children, 6–11% of school-age children experience frequent high anxiety (Bell-Dolan & Brazeal, 1993; Bowen, Offord, & Boyle, 1990; Briggs-Gowan, Horwitz, Schwab-Stone, Levanthal, & Leaf, 2000; Costello, 1989). Because the experience of anxiety is somewhat private, others may not be aware of a child's anxiety level. Certain behaviors may tip off parents and teachers that a child could be suffering from excessive anxiety (discussed below). The question is, how concerned should caregivers be if there are signs of high anxiety in school-age children? Current research provides some interesting answers to this question.

Excessive anxiety often leads to several challenges for children and their families. Most commonly, difficulties stemming from elevated anxiety are seen in the scholastic, social, and home domains (Langley, Bergman, McCracken, & Piacentini, 2004; Wood, 2006a, in press-a). High anxiety can interfere with children's cognitive abilities in academic situations, partly because their attention is divided between the task at hand and their worried thoughts about feared events (e.g., failing, being away from parents, embarrassing themselves). High anxiety is also associated with disturbance in recall of previously mastered academic knowledge (Ma, 1999). Over the course of a school year, children with high levels of anxiety may perform below their ability level, leading to lower academic performance and mastery.

In addition, social development may be harmed by elevated anxiety. Children who are highly anxious may avoid interacting with peers and teachers, or act in a less confident manner. For example, initiating conversations or joining others' activities in progress may be difficult when children are very anxious, which can prevent inclusion in the day-to-day social events that make elementary school fun and rewarding for most students. Attempting to avoid embarrassment or rejection tends to motivate this shy and reticent behavior. Excessive anxiety may also make it difficult for children to make close friends at school. Fortunately, we have found that when child

5

anxiety decreases over time, social adjustment and academic achievement tend to improve correspondingly (Wood, 2006a).

Child anxiety can also exert a negative impact upon the family (Langley et al., 2004). As discussed in detail below, counterproductive parenting practices are associated with high levels of child anxiety (McLeod, Wood, & Weisz, 2007), although this may be a result of the child's anxiety or an antecedent of the anxiety (Wood, McLeod, Sigman, Hwang, & Chu, 2003). Additionally, parents may find their lives significantly affected by child anxiety symptoms. For example, a child who refuses to go to school may cause his or her parent to miss a significant amount of work. Acute separation anxiety may make it impossible to leave a child with a babysitter due to the emotional toll it takes on all parties (e.g., children may panic, plead, cling to parents, or lash out at babysitters). Substantial family conflict may arise over suggestions given by parents or siblings to the child to act in a more courageous manner. Whatever feared or avoided situations may be in question, children with high anxiety are unlikely to engage in a rational assessment based on the type of encouragement sometimes given by family members, which can have an unintentionally critical, unsympathetic, and rigid quality (Moore, Whaley, & Sigman, 2004). In short, both the affected child and his or her family members often suffer as a result of anxiety disorders. Children may be exposed to ill will from loved ones and feel guilty and isolated, while parents and siblings may be frustrated by the restrictions imposed on them by the child's anxiety-related demands. In sum, elevated anxiety can have deleterious effects upon children's academic, family, and interpersonal functioning.

THE CONTINUUM OF FEAR, ANXIETY, AND WORRY

Fear, anxiety, and worry are closely related mental states that follow a linear progression. The continuum begins with vague concerns about distal problems associated with worry, expands to more specific anticipated threats and related discomforts of anxiety, and culminates in an overwhelming sense of imminent danger and fight-or-flight reactions characterizing fear (Craske, 1999).

Fear

Emotion theorists consider fear to be one of the primary (basic) emotions, along with sadness, disgust, interest, and anger. These emotions are evolutionarily maintained because they motivate specific adaptive behaviors essential for the survival of the species (Ekman, 1992; Fanselow, 1994; Izard, 1992). Basic emotions are triggered by prepared biological events that activate neural response systems; conscious thought or effort is not necessary to initiate an emotion (Izard, 1992). The fear response includes activation of the sympathetic nervous system (SNS), which prepares an organism for fight or flight by releasing adrenalin into the bloodstream, among other effects. In humans, research suggests that the fear response is also characterized by the subjective experience of distress and the intense desire to take action to attain a sense of safety (Craske, 1999). Fear, panic, and phobic fear are generally considered to be the same basic emotion (Barlow et al., 1994).

Anxiety

Anxiety is conceptualized as a negative mood state that is marked by some degree of SNS arousal (e.g., stomachaches), as well as a cognitive state characterized by a high level of attention to signs of threat and danger (Gunnar, 2001). The function of anxiety is to prepare the organism to counteract potential future threats. Emotion theorists assert that anxiety is characterized by cognitive associations developed via early learning experiences that connect basic emotions (fear) with specific events or meanings (Izard, 1992). For example, a young child who experienced an intense fear response (i.e., a basic emotion) when attacked by a dog (a specific event) may develop anxiety about seeing dogs in the future. Anxiety is therefore characterized by cognitive and physiological features in addition to a general state of unease or negative affect. As a perceived danger nears, there is an increase of all of these features that build up to the basic emotion of fear.

Worry

Worry is defined as thoughts and beliefs about possible problems that may occur in the future (Rapee, 2001). Compared to anxiety, worry is primarily focused upon distal events and is characterized by SNS suppression rather than arousal (e.g., Brown, Chorpita, & Barlow, 1998). The function of worry is to help individuals reduce emotional processing by focusing on future dangers and making preemptive plans and contingencies. Semantic processing (i.e., the mental self-talk that characterizes worry) may suppress SNS arousal and anxiety-producing imagery (Borkovec & Inz, 1990). Early learning situations likely influence the nature of an individual's worries by highlighting specific events that seem to represent potential threats worthy of consideration and caution in the future.

CHARACTERISTICS OF COMMON CHILD ANXIETY SYNDROMES AND DISORDERS

For the purposes of this book, the term *child anxiety disorder* is used as a convenient convention to describe a syndrome of experiences and behaviors that commonly occur together, have clinical significance, and are worthy of treatment. Anxiety disorders represent specific anxiety symptom clusters that cause significant distress or impairment. Distress is a subjective experience in which symptoms feel overwhelming or intolerable to an individual. Impairment, however, may be objectively observed by others—for instance, when anxiety prevents a child from going to school, making friends, or having a pleasant family life. Research has demonstrated that meaningful clusters of anxiety symptoms, such as social anxiety, are evident in children seeking treatment in clinical settings (Wood, Piacentini, Bergman, McCracken, & Barrios, 2002). In the following section, we describe the cardinal features of the anxiety disorders most commonly experienced by children.

Separation Anxiety

"Mommy, is there going to be an earthquake? Would your office fall over in an earthquake?" "Dad, promise you won't drive on the freeway today. I heard there was lots of accidents on Highway 5."

The most common syndrome of anxiety experienced by school-age children is separation anxiety disorder (SAD), with prevalence rates estimated at around 4% of the population (Briggs-Gowan et al., 2000; Costello, 1989). Affected children are troubled by *irrational beliefs* (i.e., worries) that they or their caregivers are in significant danger when away from one another. Children tend to ruminate over concerns about running into kidnappers, robbers, monsters, and other "bad guys" while they are away from their parents. However, these children also often worry that parents might get in a car accident or be caught in a natural disaster that would injure or kill them. In either case, the emphasis tends to be on the fact that the child and parents would never be together again. To be diagnosed with SAD, children must experience these symptoms for 4 or more weeks.

Affected children also experience anxiety as they anticipate being separated from their parents. For example, as a child is being driven to school, he or she may start to experience SNS arousal and fearful thoughts as the anticipated separation approaches. When finally faced with saying goodbye, the child may have an acute emotional response characterized by intense physiological symptoms, as well as crying, screaming, and clinging to the parent. In such a state, the child is unable to process verbal information well due to an almost complete focus on an (unrealistic) threat that seems imminent. Thus, children with separation anxiety often experience symptoms that include worry, anticipatory anxiety, and fear.

Many children are only able to verbalize some portion (or sometimes none) of their irrational thoughts until significant psychoeducation (i.e., teaching children psychological concepts—in this case, that anxious feelings are inevitably accompanied by specific types of frightening beliefs) is provided during cognitive-behavioral therapy (CBT; see Part II). Parents may be aware to some degree of such concerns based on comments or questions their children have posed to them (see above). There are many behavioral manifestations that serve to corroborate or initially suggest the existence of separation anxiety. Children affected by clinical levels of separation anxiety avoid leaving their caregivers and other family members under a variety of circumstances. In extreme situations, children like Spencer (the case example at the beginning of this chapter) may exhibit school refusal (Wood, in press-b).

Parents of children exhibiting school refusal have generally tried many methods to help their children return to school, to no avail—it is not merely deficient or laissez-faire parenting that explains their children's absenteeism (Wood, in press-b). School refusal is frequently tied to high levels of negative mood and panic, often resulting in physical symptoms such as vomiting when an attempt is made to attend school. Many families are not able to overcome it on their own (Kearney, 2003).

Less extreme manifestations of separation anxiety involve avoidance of extracurricular activities (e.g., after-school classes or sports), playdates, or casual play in the neighborhood with peers. Some children experience separation anxiety even inside their homes and trail parents around the house, staying within eyesight whenever possible. Babysitters and other alternative caregivers are often rejected because they signify that the child and parent will be away from one another, which connotes a threat. Often, nighttime rituals develop to keep separation anxiety at bay—ranging from cuddling and staying together until the child falls asleep in his or her own bed to cosleeping in the parents' bed every night (see Wood, 2006b, for a case example). Of course, cosleeping varies in frequency across cultures and is by no means a sign of problematic anxiety by itself. Nonetheless, clinicians should be aware of the difficulty that children with elevated separation anxiety would experience if required to sleep by themselves. It is this difficulty and the likelihood of a fearful response that distinguishes a run-of-the-mill cosleeper who would cheerfully sleep alone when asked from a child who must cosleep to regulate anxiety.

One interesting complexity in SAD pertains to whom the child has attached and can use as a proxy caregiver or loved one. In some cases of separation anxiety, a child may exhibit the ability to separate from parents and spend time in a particular setting (e.g., school, a public bathroom) because the child develops a relationship with someone who can serve as a safety cue. Who may serve in this role can surprise caregivers at times. For example, a fourth grader with separation anxiety may feel comfortable going into a public bathroom without his parents if his 3-year-old brother comes with him. A panic-stricken kindergartner who refuses to attend school may separate easily from parents for Sunday school because her best friend is going to be there. A sibling may also serve as an acceptable alternative to parents for cosleeping for some children with high separation anxiety. Commonly, children report feeling safe with these proxy caregivers. We have noted that the children most likely to affiliate with nonparental figures are primarily worried about their own safety rather than that of their parents. The proxy caregivers seem to provide a sense of protection for children when they are together (though from an adult's standpoint this may seem illogical).

The experience of separation anxiety is rooted in the early phases of infant development and is a reaction linked with the milestone of object permanence, which allows infants to remember their caregivers and notice their absence (Silove & Manicavasagar, 2001). Emotional processes become linked to the concept of a permanent caregiver, and distress is experienced when caregivers leave temporarily. The adaptive value of separation anxiety is clear—young children need to be protected by their caregivers and instinctively seek proximity to them by engaging in affiliative behaviors (clinging, crying) to increase visibility and avoid being left alone. The experience of anxiety when children anticipate separations from caregivers motivates children to engage in these adaptive, self-preserving behaviors. Some degree of separation anxiety is therefore functional and serves to bond family members together, enhancing safety as well as social cohesion. It is only when such anxiety becomes so intense that it prevents appropriate development in other areas of a child's life (e.g., formation of meaningful friendships) that it should be considered a problem needing treatment.

Social Anxiety (Social Phobia)

"I kinda feel shyer than other kids. I don't really know what to say." "I mostly just read a book during recess. I don't feel exactly comfortable going up to people." "It's embarrassing to have everyone staring at you, so I pretty much don't join any teams or do any of that stuff after school. It gets sorta boring, though."

Fear of public speaking is a common fear reported by youth (Morris & Masia, 1998) that epitomizes the core irrational belief underlying many cases of high social anxiety, which is that embarrassment or humiliation are likely to occur. In public speaking, this is magnified in multiple ways—all attention seems to be on the speaker, making it difficult to mask a gaffe; multiple people are observing, resulting in a potential "mass" of criticism, and, because of the public spectacle involved, there is a much greater chance of rumors circulating about a mistake, with potential implications for loss of status in an entire peer group. Because the perceived stakes are so high many individuals fall prey to public speaking anxiety. However, for an average person, this sort of anxiety primarily motivates an adaptive coping response—additional preparation—to increase the odds that the event turns out successfully. In contrast, when social anxiety is overwhelming, it may promote avoidance of various social activities or inhibit performance in social situations. Children with high social anxiety often have attentional and memory biases that influence their perception of social interactions (Morris, 2001). Such children tend to misperceive social cues and situations, with a bias toward perceiving and recalling rejection. These children also tend to remember social situations that had negative outcomes as opposed to social interactions that had positive outcomes.

As affected children anticipate facing social situations, they tend to experience anxiety, with symptoms intensifying—sometimes to a state of panic—as the situation approaches (e.g., waiting to give a book report). As a result, children with high levels of social anxiety tend to avoid many situations that would be developmentally appropriate for them. Often children are reticent to speak in class; in extreme forms, this can result in selective mutism—failure to speak at all in specific situations. Selective mutism affects approximately 0.71% of early elementary school children, is not due to a diagnosable speech or developmental disorder, and can persist over time (Bergman, Piacentini, & McCracken, 2002). Even in less extreme forms, children with a social anxiety disorder often limit their participation to the bare minimum in group discussions to keep attention away from themselves; keep to themselves rather than approach other children on the playground and in other unstructured peer situations; fail to talk on the phone except under duress; resist initiating get-togethers even with friends; and fall silent when confronted with new children or adults. There is no predictable pattern of specific social situations that will cause elevated anxiety for a given child. However, it has been noted that affected children usually have either a focal social phobia of one primary situation that causes avoidance or distress (e.g., public speaking) or a generalized fearfulness of many different social situations (e.g., interacting with peers, authority figures, extended family; American Psychiatric Association, 1994).

As with separation anxiety, children may be initially less aware of the maladaptive cognitions about danger in social situations that underlie their anxiety. However, comments made to parents and therapists when discussing reasons for avoidance (e.g., "They wouldn't like me"; "They'll think I've got a dumb voice"; "Everyone would laugh") provide a window into the thought processes that contribute to heightened anxiety and reticent behavior. As long as such beliefs are firmly rooted (either consciously or unconsciously), it is unlikely that a child will overcome social anxiety. Thus, these beliefs represent a major focus of treatment.

It is important to distinguish the social anxiety syndrome from developmental disabilities such as autism and Asperger syndrome. In most cases of social anxiety disorder, children have reasonably adequate social skills and speech and language abilities, as well as an age-appropriate motivation to form friendships and other relationships. For such children, their anxiety in social situations interferes with their ability to use appropriate social skills (e.g., they freeze when meeting a peer for the first time). In comparison, children with some developmental disabilities lack the requisite skills, abilities, and social motivation, which may lead to a pattern of social withdrawal (Rubin, Burgess, Kennedy, & Stewart, 2003) and shyness that emerges from their fundamental deficits and atypical developmental patterns, and not just from anxiety. Of course, anxiety often plays an important role in autism and

Asperger syndrome as well, and may be responsive to modified CBT procedures (Sze & Wood, in press).

Many parents ask if social anxiety is a clinical problem or merely a case of shyness, and this is a legitimate question. Like other anxiety disorders, a diagnosis of social anxiety disorder requires either substantial distress experienced by the child (e.g., frustration with a limited social life or with constant preoccupation with and dread of upcoming social events) or impairment in functioning. For example, children with high social anxiety often report having no friends (Beidel, Turner, & Morris, 1999), which can have deleterious long-term effects on the child's social development. Conversely, most children who are merely shy do not develop social anxiety disorder (Schwartz, Snidman, & Kagan, 1999). Such children often have a small, stable group of friends, are content with their social life, and thus do not require intervention.

Like separation anxiety, social anxiety has roots in early child development, and has some adaptive value. Kagan, Snidman, Zentner, and Peterson (1999) have studied an infant temperament (personality) trait known as behavioral inhibition, which involves fearfulness and withdrawal when confronted with unfamiliar situations or people. Because some unfamiliar stimuli are dangerous for children (e.g., some strangers, many substances), experiencing fear and anxiety when exposed to novel situations can be a self-preserving response. Experiencing anxiety and fear causes children to retreat to trusted caregivers to check in with them, a process called social referencing (Carver & Vaccaro, 2007), increasing the likelihood that unsafe situations (danger) will be avoided. Although some wariness around novel stimuli is common and has value in early childhood, a pattern of excessively reticent behavior that persists into middle childhood can predispose children to develop social phobia (Eisenberg, Fabes, Damon, & Eisenberg, 1998; Kagan et al., 1999).

Generalized Anxiety

"If I was tardy to class tomorrow . . . I dunno, I might get bad grades from my teacher. ['What would happen then?'] . . . I guess I might fail third grade! And have to repeat it. ['What would happen then?'] . . . Umm, well then I probably wouldn't get into a good middle school. And if I didn't get into a good middle school, I wouldn't get into a good high school or college. So then I wouldn't get a job—probably have no job. ['What would happen then?'] . . . Pretty much, I might end up homeless living in the gutter."

The generalized anxiety disorder cluster is characterized by preoccupation with a multitude of worries about daily life. Many affected children worry about their ability to achieve perfection in their schoolwork and homework. Worries may consist of thoughts such as, "What if I don't do well on the test tomorrow?" or "What if I have so much homework I cannot finish it?" Although many schoolchildren experience such worries, for affected children the anxiety associated with the thoughts is grossly out of proportion with the "threat" involved (e.g., having a somewhat lower grade than usual or receiving a few points off homework) and is thus atypical (Rapee, 2001). These children generally find it difficult to control these worries and, as a result, can experience distress, irritability, and loss of concentration, among other symptoms.

Persistent, chronic worrying about an array of topics can greatly interfere with a child's functioning. For example, for children who worry excessively about school performance, despite the fact that the ultimate goal is scholastic perfection, such worries often trigger a great deal of avoidance. Children may resist starting homework (e.g., for fear of performing inadequately) and beg not to go to school in the morning in order to avoid the stress associated with classwork. Unfortunately, avoidant behavior often increases the chance of experiencing negative consequences. Some children actually miss school because their physical anxiety symptoms make them miserable and lead their parents to keep them home. Others get into repeated, protracted conflicts with caregivers, lose sleep, or miss out on social opportunities in order to focus efforts on scholastic preparation (or worry about scholastic preparation). Thus, a child's worries tend to lead to avoidance, which serves to exacerbate the worries and place the child in a catch-22 situation.

Other common areas of generalized anxiety are worries about performance in extracurricular activities (e.g., art, music, sports), social life (e.g., one's appearance, peer group dynamics), world events (e.g., war, crime), and one's health. Children rarely experience disturbing worries in all of these domains, but due to the generalized nature of this syndrome, multiple worries that are intense and hard to stop are common among children seeking treatment.

In contrast to the separation and social anxiety syndromes, generalized anxiety often develops later in childhood. This is because worry requires higher level cognitive processes (concrete operations that permit more abstract symbolic representations of the self and the future) that develop with age. The mental act of worrying requires that an individual has the capacity to think about the future, imagine the negative possibilities that it may hold, and develop worried inner self-talk (e.g., "something bad might happen to me"). As a result, generalized anxiety disorder is typically seen in older children. It is important to note, however, that children approaching kindergarten age (4- to 5-year olds) occasionally develop a disorder with these characteristics that requires clinical attention.

Other Anxiety Syndromes

Additional patterns of fear and anxiety include phobias, panic disorder, obsessive-compulsive disorder (OCD), and post-traumatic stress disorder (PTSD). The treatment manual presented in the second half of this book was developed specifically for children with separation anxiety, social anxiety, or generalized anxiety—the most common anxiety clusters in childhood. In our clinical experience, these treatment techniques appear to be applicable to additional anxiety syndromes as well, but more research is needed to confirm this. Other programs have been developed specifically to treat phobias (Silverman et al., 1999), OCD (Pediatric OCD Treatment Study [POTS] Team, 2004), and PTSD (Cohen, Deblinger, Mannarino, & Steer, 2004).

Phobias are fears of a specific stimulus (e.g., spiders) or situation (e.g., heights) that lead to avoidance or severe distress. Children with specific phobias often come to fear that a particular stimulus will be present in many different places and therefore avoid numerous situations. As an example, a child who has a spider phobia might avoid playing outside the house, insist that his parents vacuum every room in the house on a daily basis, and refuse to go certain places where he has seen spiders in the past (e.g., the garage). Thus, although the focus of fear and anxiety in phobias tends to be very circumscribed, the interference that this condition causes can resemble the impairment associated with the other anxiety syndromes described above. In diagnosing phobias, it is important to note that some fears are common throughout childhood, such as fear of the dark (see Warren & Sroufe, 2004, for a discussion). Thus, specific phobias should not be diagnosed unless they interfere with daily functioning (e.g., going outside, getting along with family members).

Panic disorder is an anxiety syndrome that is prevalent in adults, especially women (Craske, 1999), but is rare in children (Birmaher & Ollendick, 2004). Some researchers have argued that a relatively high level of abstract thought is necessary to experience panic disorder symptoms, precluding most school-age children from developing this syndrome. Panic attacks are a physiological enactment of the fight-flight response in which autonomic symptoms (e.g., shortness of breath, racing heart) are so intense that the individual may misinterpret the symptoms as a heart attack or other serious medical condition. Although panic attacks can be present in the course of any anxiety disorder—for instance, a child with severe social anxiety may experience a panic attack moments before going on stage in front of the school—the development of fear about having panic attacks is the defining characteristic of panic disorder and requires the ability to conceptualize a psychological state (panic) distinctly enough to become preoccupied about it. This phenomenon is often referred to as *fear of fear* (Craske, 1999). Agoraphobia—the fear of going out in public places—usually develops concurrently with panic disorder. This is because individuals with panic disorder often fear that they will have a panic attack in a public place, potentiating serious injury or death due to the lack of available medical help (i.e., because the panic attack is often misinterpreted as a medical problem).

Obsessive-compulsive disorder is a distinct anxiety pattern that is fairly rare in children (2% lifetime prevalence; see Whitaker, Johnson, Shaffer, & Rapoport, 1990) but can be quite debilitating. Children may experience obsessions (upsetting thoughts that they cannot control), compulsions (repetitive rituals that ease or prevent anxiety), or both. Classically, compulsions were thought to emerge as a means of reducing obsessions, but due to developmental factors children may not be able to identify their obsessions (Franklin, Rynn, Foa, & March, 2004). Obsessions commonly focus on fears of contamination but may also involve somewhat more bizarre content (e.g., fear that touching an elderly individual would cause one to grow old; a scary mental image of killing one's father by tossing him a baseball). Young children's obsessions often have a magical quality (Franklin et al., 2004). Compulsions often involve washing, but can also include checking, ordering, counting, and hoarding (Franklin et al., 2004). With compulsions, there is often a sense of dread that if the behavior is not performed, a terrible outcome will occur. Sometimes the expected outcome is clear-cut, often involving injury or death (e.g., failure to wash sufficiently leading to contamination and death), although the expected threat can also be nonspecific but dreadful. Some children will spend hours per day engaging in obsessive thinking or compulsive rituals. On the whole, obsessions and compulsions can greatly interfere with a child's ability to function at home and school and thus can be highly impairing.

Post-traumatic stress disorder differs somewhat from other anxiety syndromes because it is related to an identifiable trauma (Vernberg & Varela, 2001). Many children experience traumas such as child abuse, exposure to violent crime, or severe accidents. Those who have had such experiences are at risk for developing PTSD—a pattern of heightened vigilance, arousal, and preoccupation with or avoidance of stimuli associated with the trauma. There can be symptoms of reexperiencing, in which the individual feels like the trauma is occurring again, which can trigger a dissociative state. Children with PTSD are often highly distressed, may engage in disruptive behavior, can experience inattention and distractibility, often have difficulty with trust and maintaining close relationships, and may seem inconsolable to caregivers at times.

OVERLAP OF ANXIETY SYNDROMES AND OTHER FORMS OF CHILD PSYCHOPATHOLOGY

It is common that children with one type of anxiety disorder will also meet criteria for a second, third, or even fourth distinct anxiety disorder (Wood et al., 2002). Furthermore, children with an anxiety disorder are likely to have one or more disorders from other domains of psychopathology, including disruptive behavior, attention deficit disorders, pervasive developmental disorders, and mood disorders (Angold, Costello, & Erkanli, 1999;

Lewinsohn, Hops, Roberts, Seeley, & Andrews, 1993; Masi, Favilla, Millepiedi, & Mucci, 2000). In particular, in clinical settings, it is rare for children to present with a pure case of anxiety and no other forms of psychopathology (e.g., conduct problems; Jensen & Weisz, 2002). Thus, when treating children with anxiety disorders it is important to determine whether they have other, co-occurring disorders so that treatment can be planned accordingly (see Chapter 3 for further discussion of treatment planning when a child has an anxiety disorder as well as other disorders).

THE NATURAL HISTORY OF ANXIETY DISORDERS

A common question raised by many parents is: If I do nothing, is my child's anxiety likely to remit on its own? In general, anxiety disorders appear to be chronic for many children. In a study of children with social anxiety disorder or overanxious disorder, the majority (63%) still met criteria for an anxiety disorder 6 months later (Beidel, Fink, & Turner, 1996). Another study found a 4- to 5-year stability rate of about 50% for anxiety disorders in children, although children sometimes met criteria for a different anxiety disorder by the time they were reassessed (Cantwell & Baker, 1989). A 50% stability rate was also reported in a prospective study of adolescents diagnosed with OCD over a 2-year span (Berg et al., 1989). Together, these findings indicate that anxiety disorders have a persistent course, though long-term stability is mostly seen in disorder status rather than a specific anxiety disorder.

Anxiety disorders in children and adolescents appear to persist into adulthood. Young adults with current anxiety disorders often had a history of anxiety earlier in life. In a sample of 992 children, over half (62%) of the 21-year-olds with a current anxiety disorder met criteria for an anxiety disorder earlier in adolescence (Newman, Moffitt, Caspi, & Magdol,

1996). An additional 19% of the youths with a current anxiety disorder met criteria for a diagnosis other than anxiety in adolescence. Hence, only 20% of 21-year-olds with an anxiety disorder had no prior diagnosis. These results suggest that young adults with anxiety problems are likely to have had previous symptoms of anxiety and, in some cases, other mental health problems. The chronic nature of anxiety disorders underscores the importance of providing effective treatment to affected children and youth.

In summary, most studies suggest that at least half of the children diagnosed with an anxiety disorder at one point in time will continue to meet diagnostic criteria for an anxiety disorder later in childhood or adolescence, suggesting that anxiety can be a chronic problem for many children.

ACCURATE ASSESSMENT OF CHILD ANXIETY SYNDROMES

Accurate assessment of child anxiety disorders represents an important first step in the treatment process. It is important to assess the nature and severity of a child's presenting problems and determine whether the child is experiencing clinically significant anxiety for several reasons. First, a thorough assessment can indicate whether a child is primarily affected by anxiety. This determination is important because the intervention program presented here is designed to treat child anxiety and is not intended for other kinds of child psychopathology. Thus, if a child is primarily afflicted by another disorder (e.g., a mood disorder such as depression), other evidence-based treatments are probably more appropriate (see Kazdin & Weisz, 2003, for a review of evidence-based treatments for youth emotional and behavioral problems). Second, a thorough assessment can play an important role in treatment. By delineating specific anxiety symptoms that are currently manifest, the intervention can address the child's clinical needs more precisely. Third, a baseline assessment allows clinicians to determine the rate and extent of improvement over the course of treatment. In the past, child anxiety disorders were difficult to diagnose reliably (Langley, Bergman, & Piacentini, 2002). However, the development of structured diagnostic interviews and psychometrically strong self-report measures have made the assessment process easier. In fact, the field is moving toward setting guidelines for evidence-based assessment, and a few general principles have been outlined (see Mash & Hunsley, 2005, for a discussion). For child anxiety, a number of tools are available to facilitate the assessment process (see Silverman & Ollendick, 2005, for a review).

Although several diagnostic instruments have been developed to help practitioners assess child anxiety, few guidelines exist to guide the selection of the appropriate tool. The psychometric quality of the available measures is the most important criterion to consider when evaluating diagnostic tools (Mash & Hunsley, 2005). Psychometric quality is based upon a measure's reliability and validity, which reflect the measure's ability to produce accurate information. Reliability refers to the consistency of a measure (Anastasi, 1988). For example, a household scale is considered reliable if it produces the same weight over repeated assessments of the same person. Validity refers to how well a measure assesses what it is supposed to assess (Anastasi, 1988). For example, a household scale is considered valid if it produces an accurate weight. In addition to these concerns, the practicality of a measure should be considered when choosing a diagnostic tool. For clinicians, one of the most important practical considerations is the cost of administering specific assessments, including the administration time, cost of the measure itself, and time required to receive adequate training (Jensen-Doss, 2005). When working with diverse populations, clinicians must also take into account whether an instrument is culturally appropriate and available in the client's native language. In the next section, different assessment tools are reviewed.

Interview Techniques

Diagnostic interviews are composed of a standard set of questions posed to the child and parents in a predetermined order (see Jensen-Doss et al., in press, for a discussion). These interviews usually consist of diagnostic modules, each designed to assess whether a child meets *DSM-IV* criteria for a specific diagnosis. Typically, these modules progress through a series of questions designed to assess the presence or absence of each symptom for a given disorder (e.g., separation anxiety disorder), as well as any additional information needed to determine diagnostic criteria (e.g., frequency of the symptom).

The most widely used diagnostic interview for childhood anxiety problems is the Anxiety Disorders Interview Schedule for *DSM-IV*: Child and Parent Versions (ADIS; Silverman & Albano, 1996). The ADIS is a semistructured interview that assesses the major anxiety, mood, and externalizing disorders experienced by school-age children. Current and previous versions of the ADIS have exhibited excellent reliability and validity (Silverman & Eisen, 1992; Silverman, Saavedra, & Pina, 2001; Wood et al., 2002) and have been sensitive to treatment-produced changes in various clinical trials (Barrett, Dadds, & Rapee, 1996; Kendall et al., 1997; Wood et al., 2006).

In administering the ADIS, practitioners review symptom and interference reports from both parent and child interviews, giving particular weight to converging reports. When symptom criteria appear to be met for a particular anxiety disorder, final decisions about diagnoses are based on the diagnostician's judgment as to whether the distress or interference that children or parents report is clinically significant and attributable specifically to the anxiety syndrome in question. In general, positive reports from either parent or child (the "or" rule) are considered sufficient for rating a criterion as present (Piacentini, Cohen, & Cohen, 1992).

The Kiddie Schedule for Affective Disorders and Schizophrenia (K-SADS) is another widely used interview with established psychometric properties that can be used in the diagnosis of anxiety disorders and other common childhood psychological problems (Kaufman et al., 1997). Note that a version of the K-SADS that is free for usage in not-for-profit clinical settings is available for download at the following Web site: www.wpic. pitt.edu/ksads/default.htm. Like the ADIS, the K-SADS incorporates data from separate interviews with children and their parents to produce a synthetic assessment of the child's overall anxiety features. This diagnostic interview has had less research attention in terms of its usage with childhood anxiety per se, but there is favorable evidence of its utility for assessing anxiety in the extant research literature. Kaufman et al. (1997) reported excellent interrater reliability and test-retest reliability at the level of "any anxiety disorder" versus "no anxiety disorder." Similarly, there was good concurrent validity at the level of "any anxiety disorder" (Kaufman et al., 1997). Furthermore, the K-SADS has been employed in several investigations of childhood anxiety, some of which have provided evidence of additional positive psychometric properties such as predictive validity (Cortes et al., 2005). When considering the practical utility of diagnostic interviews, the ADIS and K-SADS can produce reliable diagnoses but can also be costly to administer. The total time needed to administer these measures can be 2 to 3 hours. For practitioners who decide to use the ADIS or K-SADS, it is recommended that they seek training in their proper administration prior to using them clinically. This is because both the ADIS and the K-SADS are semistructured measures, so there is room for individualization of these interviews, but this flexibility increases the need for practitioner training to ensure that the instrument is used in a valid manner.

Paper-and-Pencil Techniques

Self-report measures have also proven useful for the assessment of child anxiety. The Multidimensional Anxiety Scale for Children (MASC; March, 1998) is a standardized 39-item self-report measure of anxiety yielding four factor scores. Each item is rated on a 4-point Likert-type response scale. The four factor scales were empirically derived through principal components analysis and include Social Anxiety (9 items), Separation Anxiety (9 items), Harm Avoidance (9 items), and Physical Symptoms (12 items). The MASC is arguably the best normed and psychometrically strongest broadband child anxiety rating scale currently in use (March, Parker, Sullivan, Stallings, & Conners, 1997; March, Sullivan, & Parker, 1999). More important, the MASC factor structure roughly corresponds to the *DSM-IV* anxiety disorders (March, 1998). A second useful self-report child anxiety measure is the SCARED (Birmaher, Khetarpal, Brent, & Cully, 1997).

Using self-report measures in clinical practice has pros and cons. An advantage is that they are normed, offering a means of estimating the severity of the child's anxiety compared to that of the normal child population. A second advantage is the relative ease with which such measures may be administered. Downsides of self-report measures are that they represent only one person's point of view, do not always correspond closely with parent or diagnostic assessments of child anxiety, and do not measure the amount of interference that the anxiety is causing. The last point is particularly significant in light of the important distinction between a personality trait and a disorder. Although elevated anxiety symptoms may appear to signify a clinical problem, they may be less relevant as a focus of treatment if they are not affecting the child's adaptive functioning or making him or her miserable. Thus, if self-report measures are used as a primary means of assessing anxiety, it is important to obtain collateral information about the possible interference that this anxiety causes for the child.

Screening Techniques Used in Schools and Clinical Settings

Due to its somewhat private nature, anxiety can escape the attention of parents, teachers, and even practitioners. As a result, many children in school and clinical settings will remain undiagnosed unless large-scale screening techniques are employed. In the development of prevention or early intervention programs in schools (Dadds, Spence, Holland, Barrett, & Laurens, 1997), large-scale screenings have been conducted to determine which children would be the best candidates for preventive efforts. Two techniques have been relied upon in the extant literature for such applications: self-report measures with cutoff scores and teacher nominations. As noted above, measures such as the MASC and the SCARED provide normative scores, which can serve as the basis for establishing cutoff scores for entry into clinical interventions. Often, children with T scores at or above 60 (84th percentile), 65 (93rd percentile), or 70 (97th percentile) on these types of measures might be considered for inclusion in a prevention program. Of course, false positives and false negatives are inevitable when relying on cutoff scores to indicate a child's clinical status and treatment needs (Wood et al., 2002).

A second approach that has been employed involves teacher nominations. In general education settings, this can involve asking teachers in target classrooms to nominate the three most anxious children in the class (Dadds et al., 1997). In our current research on early interventions for childhood anxiety in schools, we supplement the request for nominations with specific information for teachers about the phenomenology of childhood anxiety to help them pinpoint children who are more likely to meet our criteria. For example, our teacher nomination form states:

> Please list the names of any children in your class who display any of the following:
>
> • Is afraid that other kids will laugh at or make fun of him or her
> • Worries about getting called on in class
> • Worries about what other people will think of him or her
> • Tries to do things exactly right and is perfectionistic
> • Worries excessively about his or her school performance, or is hypersensitive to criticism
> • Has difficulty separating from parents in the morning or gets neurotic about parents picking him or her up on time after school
>
> Please list up to three children who exhibit one or more of these traits, beginning with the most anxious child you are aware of.

In our current school-based early intervention study, we assess a child's number of visits to the school nurse as a possible indicator of anxiety (e.g., reflecting avoidance related to social or separation anxiety, or as an indicator of anxiety-based somatic symptoms such as stomachaches). Children who have visited the school nurse at least seven times in a 2-month time frame are identified for further screening. We have found (on a qualitative basis) that many children with frequent visits to the nurse do have psychological adjustment issues of various kinds, but not all of them are anxiety related. For example, some children appear to be using nurse visits as an excuse to avoid class due to learning difficulties, frustration with tasks that require high levels of attention, or social relationship problems. While a fair proportion of children in this group also have anxiety, there would be a high rate of false positives if this were the only approach used to identify children who are specifically at risk for anxiety.

Developmental Considerations in Assessment

In arriving at a diagnosis of anxiety, it is important to consider a child's level of cognitive and linguistic development (Sattler, 2001). Such developmental factors influence how a child expresses and experiences specific symptoms and syndromes (Cicchetti & Toth, 1998). As a result, it is important for clinicians to consider how such factors may impact the expression of anxiety and incorporate this knowledge into their diagnostic procedures (Schniering, Hudson, & Rapee, 2000). Consider, for example, how dysphoric mood can vary with development: Children may express dysphoric mood by appearing glum or lethargic and by crying, but be unable to report on their affective state due to limited cognitive and linguistic development; adolescents express dysphoric mood via increased irritability; and adults may be more likely to talk and reflect about feeling sad (cf. Weiss & Garber, 2003). As this example illustrates, to accurately assess aspects of psychological symptoms and disorders, practitioners must be aware of how symptoms can manifest across developmental stages.

To ensure that assessment procedures are developmentally sensitive, clinicians can apply a normative developmental approach, which involves comparing symptom presentations with expected developmental processes for a child's particular age group (Silverman & Ollendick, 2005; Warren & Sroufe, 2004). The progression of fears across childhood into adolescence can serve as an example of how using a normative developmental approach can guide the diagnostic process for childhood anxiety. For typically developing children, normal fears begin with a fear of separation from caregivers in infancy, move on in childhood to a fear of social situations, and in adolescence become more generalized (Gullone, 1996). Clinicians must therefore consider anxiety diagnoses within a developmental framework. For example, when considering a diagnosis of separation anxiety, a clinician must assess whether the degree of fear is congruent with the child's developmental level. An intense fear of being separated from parental figures reflects a normative level of separation anxiety in infancy, but in adolescence is not in line with normal development and would be a potential anxiety symptom. Adopting a normative developmental approach can therefore help clinicians decide whether a given behavior is congruent with a child's developmental level or is likely to represent a symptom.

Developmental factors also affect the extent to which children have the capability of experiencing specific types of symptoms (Schniering et al., 2000; Weiss & Garber, 2003). As noted above, cognitive limitations may preclude young children from experiencing symptoms such as worry. This is because worry requires children to have developed insight or an understanding of emotion (Dadds, James, Barrett, & Verhulst, 2004), which may not fully develop until late childhood or adolescence. Such cognitive limitations must be taken into account in order to avoid attributing behaviors or complaints to psychological symptoms (such as worry) that are unlikely to fall within a child's developmental level (Klein, Dougherty, & Olino, 2005; Weiss & Garber, 2003) unless there is strong evidence that the child can and does experience the symptom.

A child's developmental level can also impact his or her ability to report on anxiety symptoms. Language development and comprehension influence children's ability to interpret and understand symptoms described to them in clinical interviews and self-report measures (Schniering et al., 2000). For example, children have been found to interpret instructions on a self-report measure of worry differently than adolescents, indicating that cognitive development impacts children's understanding of anxiety-related concepts (Dadds et al., 2004). Practitioners should therefore consider a child's level of cognitive and language development when choosing assessment tools in order to avoid miscommunication and, potentially, inaccurate diagnoses. And clearly, when working with children of all ages, it is important to avoid relying exclusively upon child self-report for assessing anxiety problems; even if such measures are used, follow-up discussions with the child are recommended to ensure that he or she actually experiences the particular types of anxiety in question.

Practitioners must also account for the fact that developmental factors can influence children's ability to describe emotion. Children usually do not have insight into internal processes and, as a result, may have difficulty expressing subjective states (Sattler, 2001). Often, young children will show behavioral signs of emotional distress, such as somatic complaints, but will remain unaware of the semantic description of their affective state (e.g., "I am feeling nervous"). Practitioners must therefore take into account how development impacts a youngster's ability to describe subjective experiences when deciding how to collect information about anxiety (e.g., behavioral observation, parent interview). Moreover, due to the potential for miscommunication between practitioners, parents, and children, it is important that clinicians clearly define the meaning of symptoms for children and parents, and encourage them to speak up if they do not understand a concept or question (Sattler, 2001). Because interview schedules such as the ADIS were written with children's comprehension levels in mind, often the wording used in such instruments provides a good starting point for inquiring about anxiety symptoms among children who are at least in early elementary school. However, particularly for children in this age group, collateral information from parents, teachers, and direct observation can be necessary for an accurate assessment.

SUMMARY

Anxiety in childhood runs the gamut from the mundane to the truly debilitating and includes numerous manifestations and variations. Separation anxiety, social anxiety, generalized anxiety, and several other variants are relatively common in school-age children. Distinguishing anxiety problems worth treating (e.g., disorders) from typical childhood fears and anxieties is an important clinical task, one that requires attention to the impact of the child's anxiety on daily functioning and well-being. Anxiety syndromes, when untreated, can be persistent and deleterious over the arc of childhood and into adolescence and beyond. Accurate assessment of these disorders is an important first step in guiding affected children toward appropriate interventions—such as the Building Confidence program presented in Part II of this book—that can set a child's emotional development on a healthier course.

CHAPTER TWO

Causes of Childhood Anxiety: Family and Genetic Influences

• •

Eloise C., an 11-year-old girl with high social anxiety, sat on her mother's lap in Dr. Grey's office during an intake interview.

"But Mommy," she said, poking her finger emphatically at her mother's shoulder, "I *have* been trying. I just don't feel *comfortable* with that group of girls. Why, oh why didn't they put me in the class with my *friends* this year?"

Mrs. C. nodded sympathetically and explained to the therapist, "Eloise feels very uncomfortable with the new group she was put with this year. She thinks they have nothing in common. But honey, have you really even *tried* to get to know them? Tell Dr. Grey the truth."

Giggling shyly, Eloise replied, "Not exactly . . . Mommy, stop!" Laughing, she added, "Not at all. But they haven't made me feel *welcome*. And they all dress . . . stuck up."

"The thing is, Eloise hasn't really made new friends since preschool. She's had this same close group of friends, who started out as our family friends, since she was very young. They act like sisters, but Eloise has always been cautious around other kids everywhere—swimming, dance, gymnastics—and she never thinks any of them could be her friends."

Eloise grinned with embarrassment and stuck her tongue out at her mother. However, she did not challenge the point. Mrs. C. ruffled her hair and continued.

"So anyway, I long ago gave up and just figured, 'Why push her if she doesn't feel ready for it?' I thought she'd kind of grow out of her shyness. I mean, I was horribly shy myself as a little girl. I thought just by comforting her and letting her go at her own pace she'd figure it out on her own. But I've had anxieties my entire life and I just decided we needed to do something about it now that it's ruining her school year."

The nature-nurture debate raises important questions about how to understand the common scenario illustrated in the above vignette. On the one hand, the mother's history of life-long anxiety might suggest that genetic factors play an important role in her daughter's anxiety symptoms. On the other hand, some aspects of the child's environment, such as the mother's parenting style, may play a contributing role. Rather than treating the issue of causality as a nature versus nurture issue, contemporary theories have increasingly focused on the likelihood of a conjoint influence of biological and environmental factors in the acquisition of fears and anxieties (Vasey & Dadds, 2001). The essence of this viewpoint is that inheriting certain biologically based traits (e.g., easily triggered SNS arousal and panic attacks) creates a susceptibility to anxiety disorders that is magnified in certain environments. As an example, if a child is inherently easily aroused and quick to develop fearfulness and also has parents that permit avoidance of developmentally important situations (e.g., interacting with new peers), she or he may be likely to develop corresponding anxiety and avoidance problems. This gene-environment inter-action model could fit the data from the above vignette as well as a purely biological or purely environmental explanation, and offers a more complex and holistic approach to under-standing the roots of child anxiety problems.

This book adopts these contemporary perspectives by assuming that most children affected by clinically significant anxiety possess certain inherited traits that predispose them to pathological anxiety. Certain circumstances, including parenting influences, affecting children with a genetic predisposition may trigger a full-blown clinical syndrome by focusing the child's natural wariness and vigilance on a particular area of concern in day-to-day life (Craske, 1999). This chapter explores some of the research findings on the causes of childhood fears and anxieties and describes a biopsychosocial model of anxiety development. This information is important in the treatment of child anxiety disorders for two reasons: first, it helps clinicians answer parents' questions about why their child has anxiety and second, it offers a rationale for the family treatment focus adopted in the Building Confidence intervention program presented later in this book.

BIOLOGICAL BASES OF CHILDREN'S FEAR AND ANXIETY

As noted earlier, fear operates at a primitive level to motivate the fight-flight response via SNS processes that are common to many species (Gunnar, 2001). The brain's amygdala helps to monitor the environment for signs of danger by analyzing perceptions and sensations, and a neural system known as the hypothalamic-pituitary-adrenocortical axis stimulates the release of cortisol and epinephrine (adrenaline) when threat is detected, allowing organisms to act rapidly to escape or face the problem head-on (LeDoux, 2000). SNS arousal is associated with increased muscle tone, heart rate, blood pressure, sweating, and respiration, among other effects. These physiological changes are presumed to serve an adaptive function. For instance, increased heart rate and blood pressure allow metabolic fuels to be carried to muscles and the brain more rapidly and thereby enhance motor functioning for fight-flight behaviors.

SNS Reactivity

Individuals with clinical anxiety tend to experience more SNS arousal than other individuals. The tendency for these individuals to experience SNS arousal is presumed to be indicative of needless activation of the fight-flight system (Gunnar, 2001; Kagan et al., 1999) based on overestimations of threat and danger. SNS reactivity refers to the tendency to develop SNS arousal more easily than other individuals (i.e., having a low threshold for arousal). Many anxiety disorders are associated with frequent symptoms of SNS arousal, such as increased heart rate or shortness of breath, which may become full-blown panic attacks. The aversive feelings elicited by SNS arousal may promote avoidance of feared stimuli and thus contribute to the maintenance of anxiety symptoms due to the sense of relief stemming from such avoidance.

Children with high anxiety tend to exhibit greater SNS reactivity to stressful tasks than other children. In two separate longitudinal studies, young children were divided into behaviorally inhibited and uninhibited groups based on their fearful responses to novel stimuli in a laboratory setting during infancy. When exposed to stressors in a lab setting (e.g., social interactions or difficult cognitive tasks with an evaluative component), inhibited children consistently displayed greater increases in heart rate in infancy, in toddlerhood, and at preschool age when compared to uninhibited children (Kagan, Reznick, & Gibbons, 1989; Snidman, Kagan, Riordan, & Shannon, 1995). Inhibited children were also more likely to go on to develop anxiety disorders (Schwartz et al., 1999). These findings are suggestive of a linkage between childhood anxiety and SNS reactivity, which could be an inherited trait that places children at greater risk for developing anxiety disorders.

Genetic Contributions

Anxiety disorders and the personality traits that are associated with anxiety (i.e., neuroticism and introversion) appear to be partially heritable (Eley, 2001). Twin studies suggest that a child's risk of developing anxiety symptoms is linked with the proportion of common genes shared with his or her twin. Identical twins, with 100% of their genes in common, should be more alike in anxiety status than fraternal twins, with only 50% of their genes in common, if there is a genetic influence on anxiety. In one study of identical twins ($n = 220$) and fraternal twins ($n = 272$), there was a stronger concordance for identical twins, suggesting that about 60–65% of the variance in trait anxiety was due to genetic factors (Hudziak, Rudiger, Neale, Heath, & Todd, 2000). Other studies have yielded similar findings (Eley, 2001). Overall, evidence suggests a significant role for heritable contributions to childhood anxiety.

LEARNING PROCESSES IN THE ACQUISITION OF FEAR AND ANXIETY

Although some children may be genetically predisposed to become anxious and fearful, not all predisposed children develop anxiety disorders. Thus, there is the question of what processes and experiences make children nervous about specific stimuli and situations. Both classical and operant learning processes play a role in the development of many fears (cf. Sweeney & Pine, 2004). According to this viewpoint, fears of specific stimuli may be initially acquired through the association of an unpleasant stimulus with a neutral stimulus (i.e., classical conditioning). For instance, a child who is bitten by a dog while walking down her block may come to associate pain with dogs, leading to a general fear of dogs. Such learning experiences are also known as traumatic conditioning and may account for the excessive, unreasonable fears experienced by some individuals (Craske, 1999).

Negative reinforcement also plays an important role in anxiety development (Ollendick, Vasey, & King, 2001). In negative reinforcement, removal of an unpleasant stimulus increases the chance that a behavior will be repeated in the future. Feared stimuli and situations tend to be avoided, and this avoidance prevents the actual experience of fear. Avoidance of specific situations is reinforced because it prevents the unpleasant fear response and leads to a sense of relief. As a result, avoidance becomes a first response to feared stimuli or situations—even when there is no real threat.

Avoidance of situations can lead to skill deficits and poor self-confidence (Rubin & Burgess, 2001). For instance, a child who is anxious about social situations and has successfully avoided public speaking throughout childhood may experience increased demands to engage in it upon entering middle school. The lack of experience with public speaking due to passive avoidance earlier in life is likely to have contributed to less well-developed public speaking skills as well as poor self-confidence (sometimes referred to as poor *self-efficacy*, the belief in one's ability to complete a specific task successfully; Bandura, 1986). With these ingredients (a history of avoidance, poor skills, and poor self-efficacy) the chance of failure or embarrassment is increased once the child is compelled to attempt public speaking in middle school, potentially leading to a vicious cycle of increasing anxiety and avoidance that may spiral toward an anxiety disorder (Rubin & Burgess, 2001).

Some fearful behaviors may be enhanced through family conversations and subtle forms of positive reinforcement. For instance, Capps and Ochs (1995) noted that agoraphobic mothers appeared to praise and reward children's fearful conversation topics and discussion of avoidant solutions, and ignore or critique courageous statements made by their children. It is possible that positive reinforcement from others may increase children's fearful behaviors.

Albert Bandura's (1986) social learning theory has also made a large contribution to the child anxiety field by illustrating how *modeling* can increase or reduce fear and anxiety. Modeling involves observing another person in a situation engaging in a behavior or experiencing an emotion that increases the likelihood that the observer will engage in a similar behavior or experiencing a similar emotion in that situation. A simple example involves a child who observes her mother grimacing and shuddering upon seeing a picture of a doctor. Through modeling, the child will have an increased chance of reacting fearfully to the picture and perhaps to actual doctors in the future. Conversations with others about their fearful experiences can also lead to fear acquisition through information transmission (Craske, 1999). In short, various learning experiences, broadly defined, appear to contribute to the development of fear and anxiety in children.

THE COGNITIVE STRUCTURE OF ANXIETY: MALADAPTIVE SCHEMATA

Contemporary theories of psychopathology also rely on the concept of *schemata*—complex mental representations of the world composed of attitudes, beliefs, perceptions, and other mental functions that are more or less conscious for an individual. This concept is broadly used throughout the cognitive sciences (Berger & Donnadieu, 2006; Fiske & Taylor, 1991), developmental psychology (Piaget & Inhelder, 1969), and various formative models of CBT (Beck, Rush, Shaw, & Emery, 1979; Brewin, 2006; Young, 1990). A schema can be conceived of as a concept embedded within a network of concepts (Fiske & Taylor, 1991). For example, the concept of fear for a psychologically minded individual might be characterized by the descriptors "negative mood," "physical symptoms such as sweating and nausea," and "avoidant behavior" and might be associated in varying degrees with the concepts of anxiety, worry, and threat.

Schemata extend along a continuum of complexity and meaningfulness, ranging from superficial, easily verbalized definitions (e.g., heuristics) to highly complex, preconscious representations that defy verbalization (Brewin, 2006). While it may take just a moment to develop a shallow schema of a phenomenon based on a definition and a few associations (e.g., fear is a feeling similar to anxiety and it happens when facing an imminent threat), it may take years of experience and reflection to develop a deep, nuanced, complex core schema to represent the actual phenomenon and thus make predictions about it under varying circumstances. An example that illustrates this point involves professional baseball. Pitchers are likely to develop largely unconscious memories for flight patterns of a baseball under combinations of varying conditions (e.g., temperature, humidity, wind direction and strength, altitude, or one's idiosyncratic emotional reactions to individual ballparks and batters). Although most players would likely find it challenging to verbalize the subtle mechanical adjustments they make in accommodating patterns of these variables to produce a consistent type of pitch (e.g., fastball on the outside corner) across a range of conditions, the core schema for that pitch provides a mental model for these conditions that optimize the probability of a successful behavior (throwing a strike; Lerda, Garzunel, & Therme, 1996). Thus, schemata are models of the world that powerfully shape perceptions and behavior, and are often partially out of conscious awareness.

What role do schemata play in psychopathology? One influential model posits that when schemata of the external and internal world are inaccurate and "wrong," mental health disorders may arise (Beck et al., 1979). In the case of anxiety disorders, individuals develop schemata that include inaccurate information about threat (e.g., the likelihood of danger or the significance of the consequences of a minor problem; Beck, 1976). Children with separation anxiety disorder, for example, may develop a schema pertaining to the concept of *being away from parents* that includes beliefs that the likelihood of untoward consequences (e.g., being kidnapped) is high. Associated cognitions might be, "I will never get to see Mom and Dad again," "I may be harmed or killed," and "I won't grow up to live the life I imagined living." The schema might include caveats such as, "I am safe as long as I am with my older siblings," or "As long as I have my cell phone and check in frequently, danger would be minimal."

Access to one's core schema can be limited, especially for children. Children might be able to spontaneously define separations as "scary" (e.g., a shallow, automatic heuristic); however, children may only be partially aware or even entirely unaware of the catastrophic chain of beliefs they harbor at deeper levels of the schema pertaining to likelihood of threat (e.g., high) and severe consequences (e.g., death) related to separations. The cognitive model asserts that inaccurate and sometimes catastrophic cognitions contained within the schema are often responsible for maladaptive emotional and behavioral responses (Beck, 1976). For example, a child possessing a catastrophic schema pertaining to being away from parents is liable to experience panic and fear when separation is imminent and thus engage in corresponding fight-flight behavior (e.g., refusing to leave, clinging, lashing out) designed to prevent the feared consequence (predicted by the schema) from coming to pass.

In brief, the cognitive sciences have advanced significantly in recent decades and offer a model of anxiety that integrates a variety of mental processes and associated emotions and behaviors. Modern CBT relies heavily on this model of anxiety (see Chapter 3).

THEORIES OF PARENTAL CONTRIBUTIONS TO CHILDHOOD ANXIETY

Gottman, Katz, and Hooven (1997) propose that emotion regulation strategies (e.g., self-soothing, attention shifting, avoidance) may be learned during childhood from parents and could influence children's developmental pathways. From this viewpoint, parental caregiving behavior and modeling of coping skills may affect children's ability to regulate fear and anxiety. Numerous theories suggest how parental caregiving behavior might specifically influence the development of anxiety in children (cf. McLeod et al., 2007; Wood et al., 2003).

Interactions with parents may predispose children toward more or less fear and anxiety through basic learning mechanisms (e.g., modeling) as well as through effects that parental behavior may have on the development of children's emotion regulation skills. Two specific dimensions of parental communication behavior have been hypothesized to be crucial for the development of anxiety and, conversely, emotion regulation skills: parental warmth/acceptance and control/intrusiveness.

First, in traditional conceptions of parenting behavior, *warmth* refers to parental behaviors that communicate acceptance of the child's feelings and behaviors, such as active listening and praise (Maccoby, 1992). At the polar opposite of warmth are *aversive* parental behaviors such as criticism or sarcasm, excessive discipline, and rejection. Parents who communicate in a warm and accepting manner and demonstrate tolerance of children's expressions of negative affect—rather than criticizing or minimizing children's feelings—may promote the development of children's emotion regulation strategies by allowing children to learn, through trial and error, to tolerate negative affect (Gottman et al., 1997).

Second, contemporary models of childhood anxiety posit that parental intrusiveness (also referred to as high psychological control or low autonomy granting) can trigger the development of child anxiety disorders (Chorpita & Barlow, 1998; Craske, 1999; Fox, Henderson, Marshall, Nichols, & Ghera, 2005; Rapee, 2001; Wood, 2006c). Parents who act intrusively tend to take over tasks that children are (or could be) doing independently and impose an immature level of functioning on their children (Carlson & Harwood, 2003; Egeland, Pianta, & O'Brien, 1993; Ispa et al., 2004). When defining parental intrusiveness, it is important to consider both the parent's behavior and the developmental level of the child since parent-child interactions that are commonplace for certain age groups can become atypical later in childhood. Among school-age children (i.e., 6- to 13-year-olds), parental intrusiveness can manifest in at least three domains: unnecessary assistance with children's daily routines (e.g., dressing), infantilizing behavior (e.g., using baby words, excessive physical affection), and invasions of privacy (e.g., when parents open doors without knocking; Wood, 2006c).

Whereas a low level of parental intrusiveness is hypothesized to foster children's perceptions of control and mastery (Chorpita & Barlow, 1998), heightened intrusiveness is hypothesized to cause or maintain elevated levels of child anxiety (Fox et al., 2005; Rapee, 2001; Wood et al., 2003). Substantial research has illustrated linkages between self-efficacy (feelings of competence) and anxiety regulation (Bandura, 1997; Muris, 2002). In brief, intrusive parental behaviors could lessen children's self-efficacy and, hence, raise anxiety.

Particularly for children with a high initial level of anxiety (e.g., those with anxiety disorders or a temperamental disposition typified by resistance to extinction), intrusive parenting could reduce opportunities for children to face situations that they fear and tend to avoid, thus unintentionally promoting the maintenance of children's fears and anxieties. This is because such children are unlikely to habituate to (get used to) anxiety-provoking situations before intrusive parents take over tasks for them or remove them from the situation (e.g., a child who is very fearful at the start of kindergarten and is subsequently kept at home by her parents). In either case, the normal anxiety reduction process is disrupted and a reduction of the fearful response is not achieved. Thus, intrusive parenting may reduce children's sense of self-efficacy and reduce their opportunities for habituation to novel and feared situations, both of which may increase anxiety levels and possibly help sustain anxiety disorders.

SUMMARY: A BIOPSYCHOSOCIAL MODEL OF ANXIETY DEVELOPMENT

Emerging theory and research have illustrated multiple mechanisms that influence fear and anxiety in children. In contrast to traditional single-factor theories that invoke either genetic determinism or parent blaming when explaining childhood anxiety, the contemporary view is that various processes work together to shape the degree and nature of fear and anxiety experienced by a child at any one time. A biopsychosocial conceptualization of child anxiety that we have found useful in helping families understand the why question—why the child has developed such severe anxiety—stems from this view.

Our answer to parents' questions about the origins of anxiety is that some children seem to come into the world with a temperament or disposition that involves being wary and cautious, easily startled, and slow to warm up in new situations. Children with this temperament are more likely to see danger when there is none because their brain has a fairly low threshold for perceiving threat and reacting fearfully. As a result, these children develop fears more easily than others do and build up irrational, negative beliefs about various situations. Some of these children experience more intense, unpleasant physical arousal when they become fearful or anxious than do children without this temperament. These more intense negative feelings cause children to avoid challenging situations, because avoidance reduces anxiety and can generate a sense of relief. These basic temperament traits seem to be strongly influenced by genetic factors that parents had no control over. Over time, certain experiences that these children have at school, in public, or at home may focus their fears on particular concerns and problems, such as separation or humiliation. Some children become so preoccupied with a perceived threat in these situations that they are often miserable or begin to avoid the situation entirely. At this point, the child's level of fear and anxiety has escalated to the level of a psychological disorder and often requires intervention.

CHAPTER THREE

Evidence-Based Practices and Clinical Considerations

• •

PJ turned white when the therapist uttered *the word*. "Just so you know, I might run when I see it," he warned.

"PJ, I'd like you to remind me of your KICK plan. Our plan isn't to run today. Our plan is to be brave. How can we be brave with the KICK plan?"

"K . . . I know I'm nervous because I'm all jittery. I . . . my icky thoughts are—raccoons bite people! He might bite my favorite character! He might get rabies."

The therapist smiled. He knew this was an honest concern, even though the stimulus was just a picture of a raccoon. PJ was not prevaricating.

PJ continued, "Okay, C step . . . my calm thought is that this is just a picture! I never heard of a raccoon jumping out of a picture."

"Do you have any calm thoughts about your favorite character?"

"That he's too fast for the raccoon . . . that the raccoon is probably afraid of him too . . . that the raccoon's never bitten him before so why would he now?"

The therapist chuckled and gave PJ a high-five. "Okay, so what's the second K step?"

PJ grinned. "Keep practicing! Just do it!"

"Right! So, what do you think about running now? Do we need to run? Is there any reason to run?"

"No!"

"What can you say to yourself about running?"

"Running is for warthogs and meerkats! Lions don't run!" [referring to *The Lion King*]

"Okay, so you're ready?"

"Ready!"

Cognitive-behavioral therapy has been found to be efficacious in the treatment of child anxiety disorders in numerous clinical trials (Barrett et al., 1996; Kendall, 1994; Kendall et al., 1997; Wood et al., 2006). The first comprehensive CBT program, the Coping Cat intervention (Kendall, Kane, Howard, & Siqueland, 1990), set a new standard of excellence for the treatment of childhood anxiety disorders. Previous treatment programs for children had focused on eradicating specific fears or anxiety-related problems (e.g., school refusal) but had not offered a comprehensive treatment approach capable of addressing the major child anxiety syndromes such as separation anxiety disorder, generalized anxiety disorder, and social anxiety disorder. Kendall's program was thorough and flexible, and addressed each of these debilitating childhood anxiety disorders (or combinations of them) equally well. Most current child-focused CBT programs are based on the Coping Cat program.

In general, child-focused CBT programs for youths with anxiety disorders involve teaching children (1) to identify their anxious feelings and physiological signs of anxiety; (2) to identify their anxiety-provoking cognitions; (3) to develop a plan to guide coping—a plan that involves changing their thoughts (into positive self-talk) and actions (e.g., practicing in advance); and (4) to evaluate their performance and administer self-rewards. The therapist uses modeling (e.g., self-disclosure or sharing successful coping experiences), role-playing, relaxation training, and contingent reinforcement (e.g., for trying therapeutic tasks) in developing these four themes (Kendall et al., 1990). These skills are used in planning for *exposure tasks*, which play a key role in the amelioration of fear and anxiety, wherein repeated exposure to a feared (but benign) stimulus leads to a reduction in the strength of the fear response (Rachman, 1990). The primary mechanism of action believed to be responsible for anxiety reduction in CBT is exposure therapy (Ollendick et al., 2001).

Child-focused CBT programs for youth anxiety disorders have received extensive empirical support (Kendall, Aschenbrand, & Hudson, 2003). Across multiple clinical trials, research indicates that over 50% of patients no longer meet criteria for their intake primary anxiety disorder diagnosis following treatment completion (Kendall et al., 1997). It is important to note, however, that one third to one half of children continue to have clinically significant anxiety problems when treated with child-focused CBT. As a result, some investigators have raised the question of whether involving the family in CBT might bolster the success rate. The evidence suggests that broadening the scope to include the family may improve youth clinical outcomes (Barrett & Shortt, 2003). In this chapter, research support for family-based CBT—and the Building Confidence program in particular—is reviewed, followed by an overview of the CBT and family therapy techniques that have been found to be efficacious.

RESEARCH FINDINGS ON FAMILY-BASED CBT INTERVENTIONS

Family-based CBT has consistently yielded a high proportion of treatment responders (often more than 70%) and in some studies has outperformed CBT programs that primarily focus on working with the child. Several different family-based CBT interventions have been developed, which have focused on teaching parents and children problem-solving communication techniques, anxiety management strategies, and behavioral interventions (e.g., exposure, use of rewards; Barrett et al., 1996; Silverman et al., 1999). To date, seven studies have compared family-based CBT programs with child-focused CBT programs (Barrett, 1998; Barrett et al., 1996; Cobham, Dadds, & Spence, 1998; Mendlowitz et al., 1999; Nauta, Scholing, Emmelkamp, & Minderaa, 2003; Spence, Donovan, & Brechman-Toussaint, 2000; Wood et al., 2006). Five of these studies reported some outcome measures favoring family-based CBT over child-focused CBT at the posttreatment assessment, whereas no outcome measures have favored child-focused CBT over family-based CBT. Interestingly, some longer term outcome studies have suggested that differences between family-based CBT and child-focused CBT lessen over the course of years following therapy termination, but it is not clear if this is due to maturation, an effect of repeated assessments, or a true convergence of treatment outcomes (Barrett, Duffy, Dadds, & Rapee, 2001).

The Building Confidence program is a family-based CBT program for youths with anxiety disorders. In keeping with classical strategic and structural family therapy traditions (Minuchin & Nichols, 1994; Tolan & Mitchell, 1989), this program was designed to target patterns of parent-child communication and family boundaries associated with youth anxiety (Wood et al., 2003). This intervention technique was evaluated in a clinical trial in which it was compared with traditional child-focused CBT (Wood et al., 2006). Forty children with anxiety disorders (6- to 13-year-olds) were randomly assigned to family-based CBT or child-focused CBT. Anxiety disorders (separation anxiety disorder, social phobia, or generalized anxiety disorder) were confirmed by an independent evaluator using the ADIS diagnostic interview. The two treatment conditions were matched for therapist contact time (12 to 16 therapy sessions). Outcome measures included independent evaluators' diagnoses on the ADIS and improvement ratings on the Clinical Global Impressions scale; child reports on the MASC; and parent reports on the MASC (see Chapter 1). Both treatment groups showed statistically significant improvement on all outcome measures, but family-based CBT provided additional benefit over and above child-focused CBT on most indices of improvement. Highlights of the results included (a) 79% of children in family-based CBT met Clinical Global Impressions criteria for good treatment response, compared with only 26% of children in child-focused CBT; (b) children in family-based CBT had greater improvement on independent evaluators' ratings on the ADIS Clinician's Rating Scale than children in child-focused CBT; (c) parent reports of child anxiety on the MASC, but not children's self-reports, were lower in family-based CBT than child-focused CBT at posttreatment. Family-based CBT appeared to be equally effective for children with primary diagnoses of separation anxiety disorder, social phobia, and generalized anxiety disorder. In short, the extant evidence suggests that various family-based CBT treatments are robust, yielding a high rate of significant improvement within a fairly short amount of time.

In the remainder of this chapter, we describe the rationale for the cognitive, behavioral, and family therapy techniques that are used in the Building Confidence program. The specific therapeutic procedures associated with these techniques are presented in full detail in Part II of this book. Below, the theoretical and empirical basis of the program is described.

CORE COGNITIVE BEHAVIORAL STRATEGIES IN THE BUILDING CONFIDENCE PROGRAM

Comprehensive CBT programs for children have generally used a core set of cognitive and behavioral strategies that are linked with an acronym to help children remember their new coping skills (cf. Kendall et al., 1990). The Building Confidence program uses KICK as its acronym (see the example with PJ at the beginning of this chapter). The first step, K—Knowing I'm Nervous—reminds children to pay attention to their personal cues of fear and anxiety (e.g., physical sensations associated with SNS arousal such as stomachache) in order to recognize when a situation has made them anxious. The second step, I—Identify Icky Thoughts—entails identifying fearful, unrealistic beliefs about the anxiety-provoking situation. The third step, C—Calm Your Thoughts—amounts to cognitive restructuring or "finding a calmer way of thinking about the situation." The final step, K—Keep Practicing—reminds children to face their fears in order to learn that they can handle them. The CBT techniques associated with the four steps of the KICK plan are also referred to as emotion education, identifying maladaptive schemata, cognitive restructuring, and exposure therapy, respectively.

Emotion Education, Identifying Maladaptive Schemata, and Cognitive Restructuring

Many child psychotherapy programs include an emotion education component, which typically involves helping children distinguish among the basic emotions and identify their own internal cues, such as physical sensations, that indicate specific emotions are building up. The Building Confidence program emphasizes identification of physical cues associated with SNS arousal that help children recognize that they have become anxious or afraid because they are concrete, tangible aspects of anxiety easily understood by school-age youngsters. The point emphasized is that children will not know that they need to use their coping skills unless they recognize that they are afraid of something. Hence, identification of physical cues of anxiety is described as "Knowing I'm Nervous" in the KICK plan.

A primary goal of CBT addressed in the KICK plan is altering inaccurate schemata that needlessly trigger anxious reactions for the child. For example, children with separation anxiety need to develop schemata that accurately represent the degree of threat in typical separation situations (e.g., going to school). Associated catastrophic cognitions need to be challenged by developing more realistic cognitions, such as, "Certain grown-ups like teachers can keep me safe, too," or "I can stay safe when I sleep in my room by myself." However, current schemata are probably permanent memory records and cannot simply be deleted by acquiring new information (Brewin, 2006). Rather than attempting to alter existing schemata, CBT therapists employ several techniques to develop alternative, more realistic schemata that will compete with and, hopefully, overshadow the catastrophic schemata currently dominating the child's view of feared situations. In this regard, it is rarely enough to just tell a child how to modify his or her schema (e.g., "Don't worry, everything will be fine," "You have a bright future, be happy").

A core CBT strategy for building up new, realistic schemata is targeting cognitive distortions and attempting to help the individual create memorable views of the world that are more realistic and positive (Brewin, 2006). In the first phase, the child actively works to identify his or her maladaptive schemata ("icky thoughts," the I step). Fruitful discussions may occur in which guided questioning and modeling are used to help children deepen their understanding of how they interpret specific situations and what they fear may happen. The second phase involves encouraging children to reconceptualize a situation and generate realistic ("calm") thoughts to compete with their current unrealistic fearful interpretations and beliefs (the C step).

Cognitive restructuring is an active process that involves engaging in a series of related mental processes (synthesis and analysis of personal experiences and memories; comparison of fearful beliefs to "factual" information; deduction of principles about the nature of feared situations and the status of the unrealistic fearful beliefs; and generation of language to summarize these ideas). Conjointly, these processes create (a) greater awareness of the depth and content of one's own schema; and (b) new beliefs and associations that, with sufficient rehearsal under appropriate conditions for creating unique and retrievable memories, are more likely to be recalled in challenging situations than older inaccurate schemata (Brewin, 2006).

Often the therapist stimulates this type of thinking by posing carefully worded questions that include clues to promote reflection and insight and that guide the child in the right direction but do not provide the exact answer (Socratic questions). An example of a Socratic question that might be used early in therapy is, "How could a kid remind herself that it is not very likely that she would drown in the shallow end of the pool?" This type of wording helps children focus their thoughts on evidence consistent with the stated parameter of "not very likely" and commonly evokes responses such as, "She could remind herself that she has never heard of someone drowning in the shallow end, and anyway it would be almost impossible because your head is above water!" This carefully worded question provides the child with direction as to the types of evidence to consider in search of helpful calm (realistic) thoughts. The question offers ways of thinking about fears (e.g., focusing on likelihood) that tend to help in the process of cognitive restructuring. Comparatively, non-Socratic, nonguiding questions such as, "What would be a good calm thought?" early in therapy can generate generic or inappropriate responses such as, "That she would be okay," or "That she could call for help," that do not reduce anxiety because they are not legitimate solutions to the perceived dangers.

Because the Building Confidence program is designed for school-age children, it makes extensive use of cartoons depicting common anxiety-producing situations that can facilitate the process of identifying and restructuring maladaptive schemata.

For school-age children, cartoons can focus attention upon therapeutic content (e.g., anxiety-provoking situations) without overly emphasizing the child's personal anxieties (which are often best discussed in moderation to avoid embarrassment and resistance). Children can write in "thought bubbles" for the cartoon characters' catastrophic thoughts when they are learning to identify unrealistic beliefs associated with anxious situations. Similarly, children can practice cognitive restructuring by writing in calm thoughts for the cartoon characters. Therapists are also encouraged to use self-disclosure and modeling of icky thoughts and calm thoughts to facilitate the identification and restructuring process.

Correcting Inaccurate Schemata Using Hands-on Experience

Cognitive restructuring by itself is often not enough to yield clinical change in children (Kendall et al., 1997; Ollendick et al., 2001). Constructivist models of learning have long emphasized the need for individuals to develop accurate schemata through hands-on experience and work with a phenomenon (Brewin, 2006; Piaget & Inhelder, 1969). The term *work* implies manipulation and observation of a phenomenon under varying conditions. Imagine a preschool student developing a conceptualization of sand. Compared to talking about sand in the abstract, a child gains far more information by actively touching and playing with sand (ranging from easily articulated descriptions such as "rough" to unconscious sensory memories of the weight, stickiness, and texture of sand, how it feels as it runs between the fingers, and so on). Information gained through experiential activities adds considerably to the accuracy of the overall mental model of a concept, even if these descriptors defy easy verbalization. As a result, most learning paradigms for school-age children in contemporary education incorporate substantial hands-on experience to mediate optimal comprehension and mastery

(Puntambekar & Kolodner, 2005). Direct experiential learning is also emphasized in CBT to enhance schema acquisition.

For example, rather than spending countless hours talking with children about how to return to school in cases of school phobia, a CBT program that emphasizes increasingly long visits to school (i.e., hands-on experience) can mediate a rapid reduction of anxiety and return to full-time attendance (Blagg & Yule, 1984). According to the cognitive model underlying CBT, this is because such direct experience offers corrective information that addresses nonverbalized but influential components of the client's schema that contribute to his or her inappropriate emotional and behavioral responses. In short, cognitive restructuring and hypothetical role-playing can raise a child's awareness of the unexpressed beliefs and associations at the deeper levels of an inaccurate schema but are unlikely to challenge these beliefs by themselves. However, direct experience with relevant situations can help promote development of competing, positive schemata by providing a greater volume and variety of corrective information (i.e., both verbal and nonverbal, at both conscious and implicit levels of memory) that is contextually relevant and more likely to be recalled when faced with the same type of context in the future (Brewin, 2006).

Exposure therapy is a key treatment component of CBT. This component represents the behavioral (hands-on) aspect of the treatment and can be understood in terms of basic learning processes. Just as associative and operant learning processes may contribute to the development of fears, the same processes are hypothesized to play a role in the reduction of fear. Facing feared situations can lead to *habituation* and *extinction*—basic learning processes in which repeated exposure to a stimulus that is feared but safe (e.g., attending school, staying with a babysitter, speaking with a new peer) leads to a reduction or elimination of the fear response (Rachman, 1990). The Building Confidence program uses gradual exposure to help children face feared situations. With this approach, each child makes a *fear hierarchy*, which is a list of a range of anxiety-provoking situations ordered from mild to severe. Using the skills learned earlier in the program, the child slowly works his or her way up the fear hierarchy, gaining self-confidence as lower level fears are mastered and tackling more challenging situations until the processes of habituation and extinction curb or eliminate fear in most settings.

Because facing feared situations is often difficult for children, positive reinforcement plays an important role in CBT for youth anxiety. Children are sometimes unmotivated to participate in the exposure therapy portion of treatment. Properly timed positive reinforcers (e.g., praise or points for a reward system) can increase motivation to face feared situations, permitting habituation and extinction to occur. The program emphasizes family discussions to develop collaboration among all participants on facing specific fears and setting up and maintaining a reward system that motivates children to face fears because they know that they will have something positive to look forward to.

The program begins by teaching children the KICK plan over the course of four sessions; only then does exposure therapy begin in earnest. The cognitive therapy components of CBT generate an outline for the exposure therapy experiences to fill in, creating a dynamic interactive process between cognitive and behavioral CBT techniques. Through the process of assimilation, schemata maintain integrity and continuity by filtering new information and experiences to be consistent with the expectations and beliefs that they embody (Piaget & Inhelder, 1969). For example, children with relational schemata characterized by insecure attachment often misconstrue the actions of others as threatening or rejecting (Wood, Emmerson, & Cowan, 2004). Consequently, if exposure therapy experiences (i.e., facing feared situations) are conducted without initial cognitive work (i.e., identifying maladaptive schemata and developing the outlines of positive competing schemata), children's negative expectations about these situations might simply be confirmed because contradictory evidence is overlooked or explained away through the assimilation process. Cognitive restructuring offers a rudimentary alternative framework for children to work from that represents a possibly accurate alternative mental model of a situation or concept that is worthy of further exploration and testing.

Helping children explore their maladaptive beliefs and develop corresponding positive beliefs provides specific hypotheses to test during experiential learning opportunities like exposure therapy. As an example, rather than sending a scared child back to school for 30 minutes a day without any mental preparation—likely resulting in escalation of negative affect by the process of assimilation noted above—the CBT approach involves partnering with the child, encouraging him or her to take an active role in (1) identifying thoughts that might contribute to anxious feelings; (2) developing initial realistic thoughts about the planned behavioral experience to gain self-efficacy and a sense of control; (3) adopting a scientific attitude by comparing existing inaccurate beliefs with the information gained during the hands-on experience; and (4) after returning to school for an agreed-upon length of time, reflecting on which hypothesis was supported by the experiential evidence, helping to consolidate the meaning of the experience through deep (analytical) processing of the event. Thus, the cognitive and behavioral components of CBT work synergistically to promote positive schemata that are likely to be recalled in future feared situations in a manner that neither component could accomplish alone.

FAMILY INVOLVEMENT IN THE BUILDING CONFIDENCE PROGRAM

The integration of the family into the therapeutic tasks in the Building Confidence program is critical. Parents can be helpful to children in fearful situations by prompting them to use coping skills, such as the KICK plan, to promote courageous behavior rather than giving in to automatic impulses to escape. Moreover, many exposure tasks must be done as homework (e.g., returning to school, staying in rooms by oneself at home, having playdates with new peers). Although it may be possible to forge an agreement between child and therapist on specific therapeutic tasks to accomplish outside the session, two factors may hinder the child's follow-through if parents are not involved in the planning and execution of these tasks. First, children, even with the best intentions, often forget to engage in exposure tasks when they are required to remember to do them on their own. Second, parents often play an important role in facilitating exposure opportunities (e.g., taking children to school for a specific amount of time; allowing children to sleep in their own room; hosting playdates). If parents are not consulted and brought into the planning process for home-based exposure tasks, they will not know what role to play and may not find the tasks feasible. For this reason, planning for exposure tasks requires repeated family discussions using a problem-solving format that enhances feelings of control and collaboration among all family members.

As noted in Chapter 2, parental intrusiveness may affect childhood anxiety by influencing children's opportunities for habituation and extinction. Parents who act intrusively are posited to interfere with habituation by preventing children from actually confronting feared stimuli (Fox et al., 2005; Rapee, 2001). For example, the parents of a child who freezes when faced with unfamiliar peers (a common symptom of social anxiety) might speak for the child, rub the child's shoulders, hold his hand, and remain very close to him in an attempt reduce the child's negative affect. Though effective for reducing the child's anxiety in the short term, if such parenting practices persist over time they may unintentionally prevent the child from habituating to the setting by keeping him from learning there is nothing to be afraid of. Additionally, this response may induce dependence on the parents for external emotion regulation (e.g., "I only feel comfortable around new kids when Mom and Dad are there"). Conversely, parents who grant autonomy (e.g., slowly encouraging the child to interact more and more with peers; refraining from physical or verbal comforting) may promote habituation and thus contribute to the amelioration of child anxiety symptoms. Though a high level of intrusiveness may contribute to the continuation of a child anxiety disorder, reducing intrusiveness could lead to improvement in a child's anxiety symptoms.

The program directly intervenes with parental intrusiveness and autonomy granting, with the goal of enhancing the effects of traditional child-focused CBT. Its family interventions emphasize (a) giving choices when children are indecisive (rather than making choices for them); (b) allowing children to struggle and learn by trial and error (rather than taking over tasks for them); (c) labeling and accepting children's emotional responses (rather than criticizing them); and (d) promoting children's acquisition of novel self-help skills. Each of these family intervention techniques is consistent with strategic and structural family therapy approaches that emphasize altering communication patterns in the family and improving boundaries among family members (Minuchin & Nichols, 1994; Tolan & Mitchell, 1989). Potential enmeshment between parents and children is addressed in a tactful manner with the focus on independence in self-help skills (see Session 4 in Chapter 4) and developing more mature roles in the family (Optional Module B in Chapter 4). Although parents are never directly confronted about their own role in providing excessive help in private daily routines (i.e., gratifying an emotional need of the parent) in the program, the rationale presented for granting children autonomy in these situations often motivates parents to change their role from peer to coach. These sessions and modules help parents see that their child can feel more self-confident if he or she is encouraged to adopt more independence and more mature roles, and that the parents can actively facilitate these changes through their own parenting behaviors.

Teaching parents to use these strategies also engages them in the CBT treatment philosophy and helps them provide therapeutic support during the child's exposure tasks (facing fears). Interventions aimed at reducing parental intrusiveness facilitate these sorts of exposure tasks by ensuring that parents are comfortable with their children experiencing some degree of negative emotion, that they do not take over such tasks for their children or permit avoidance, and that they provide responses to children (e.g., giving choices) that promote adaptive behavior and emotion regulation.

At a deeper level, these parenting strategies have the potential to affect children's feelings of mastery, control, and self-efficacy—self-schema that are posited to affect children's experiences of anxiety (Bandura, 1997; Chorpita & Barlow, 1998; Muris, 2002). We have hypothesized that when parents promote their children's sense of independence (e.g., allowing them to work through challenging tasks on their own; offering them choices) and grant them autonomy in self-help tasks, children have more opportunities to experience mastery and control (Wood, 2006c). Through these experiences, children are hypothesized to more readily develop self-efficacy, which is believed to promote anxiety reduction. The program aims to achieve these objectives by emphasizing the acquisition of parenting skills.

COMORBIDITY AND TREATMENT EFFICACY

Some critiques of manual-based treatments for child emotional and behavioral problems have asserted that these manuals are not designed to address comorbid diagnoses, which diminishes the value of these treatments for most clients (cf. Weisz, Jensen, & McLeod, 2005). However, evidence has not borne out this concern for children with anxiety disorders. Several studies of evidence-based treatments for child anxiety disorders have found that comorbid disorders do not seem to interfere with the successful treatment of anxiety-related problems (Kendall et al., 2003). Furthermore, both mood and disruptive behavior problems have been found to improve substantially in the context of high-quality anxiety-focused treatment (Barrett et al., 1996; Kendall, 1994).

A prioritizing approach can offer practitioners direction in selecting the most appropriate treatment manual for a given case when faced with comorbidity. For example, a child with significant anxiety who also engages in delinquent behavior most likely needs an intervention that addresses delinquency first due to its dangerousness and legal implications. An evidence-based treatment approach can be selected and implemented that addresses this area of psychopathology (Henggeler & Lee, 2003). And when the disruptive behavior symptoms remit, the need to treat any remaining anxiety can be determined. On the other hand, a child with chronic low-grade depression who also refuses to go to school due to separation anxiety will most likely require an initial treatment focus that addresses anxiety problems, since those problems likely underlie the child's absenteeism and thus account for the child's greatest area of maladjustment. Once the acute anxiety-related disturbance has been addressed, consideration of the need to implement a separate depression treatment can occur. Through this prioritizing approach, practitioners may address the realities of comorbidity by flexibly implementing a series of evidence-based treatment manuals that match a child's most pressing clinical needs.

ADAPTING THE BUILDING CONFIDENCE PROGRAM TO VARYING CULTURAL PRACTICES

One of the great strengths of the United States is its diversity. For example, in California, over one third of all public school students are Mexican American. Furthermore, 25% of all California students are English learners, and three quarters of those are Spanish speaking (cf. Rumberger & Gandara, 2004). According to the 2001 U.S. Census, foreign-born immigrants have increased more than 57% between 1990 and 2000 (U.S. Census Bureau, 2001). For mental health professionals, such diversity brings with it the opportunity to serve children from a variety of cultural backgrounds; it is critical that mental health care is provided in a competent and confident manner.

The multicultural counseling perspective asserts that effective counseling requires careful consideration of the cultural groups being served (Sue, 1977; Suzuki, Alexander, Lin, & Duffy, 2006). In an attempt to adapt counseling techniques to the needs, values, and characteristics of specific cultures being served, it is advised that culture-specific adaptations be considered (Hwang, 2006; Hwang, Wood, Lin, & Cheung, 2006; Turner, 2000). Beginning with the supposition that people of all cultures experience mental health problems, this perspective emphasizes the notion that how such problems are experienced, expressed, and defined within particular cultural groups may vary (Varjas, Nastasi, Moore, & Jayasena, 2005). According to Varjas and colleagues, "using this integrated approach one can construct . . . interventions specific to each cultural (local) setting, thus ensuring cultural specificity while maintaining focus on universal elements" (p. 244).

Several frameworks have been developed to guide cultural adaptations for counseling and psychotherapy. Most recently, Hwang (2006) developed the Psychotherapy Adaptation and Modification Framework (PAMF), which provides a set of recommendations that can be applied across multiple cultural groups. The PAMF cultural adaptations are grouped into six domains, including (1) dynamic issues and cultural complexities; (2) orienting clients to psychotherapy and increasing mental health awareness; (3) understanding cultural beliefs about mental illness, its causes, and what constitutes appropriate treatment; (4) improving the client-therapist relationship; (5) understanding cultural differences in the expression and communication of distress; and (6) addressing cultural issues specific to the population. A number of adaptation principles described in this literature can help mental health providers deliver more culturally competent and sensitive care when working with culturally diverse children with anxiety disorders (Hwang et al., 2006).

A key consideration in the development of appropriate cultural adaptations is the family's level of acculturation. Acculturation is commonly defined as the "phenomena which result when groups of individuals having different cultures come into continuous first-hand contact with subsequent changes in the original culture patterns of either or both groups" (Redfield, Linton, & Herskovits, 1936, p. 149). Individuals who are highly acculturated tend to adopt the cultural practices of the dominant society (including use of the mainstream language), while those who are less acculturated tend to retain many of the traditions practiced in their former country, including primary use of its language.

If family members have limited proficiency in English, it is crucial to find practitioners who are capable of conversing in the family's primary language, or, if such practitioners are not available, efforts must be made to enlist a good translator.

Understanding each family member's level of acculturation can aid the clinician's conceptualization of the family and potentially strengthen the working alliance with the family. It can be beneficial to ask about the family's background, when they immigrated to the United States, why the family decided to come here, and hardships that the family may have encountered during the migration process and after their arrival. During early discussions, it may be helpful for practitioners to self-disclose personal experiences aimed at increasing a sense of commonality and normalizing the family's experience (Hwang et al., 2006). The practitioner may share information about being from the same country (if relevant), having a similar family background, or having gone through the same difficulties learning English. Spending some extra time talking about these issues helps family members feel understood and sets the stage for a collaborative relationship.

Similarly, by learning about a family's cultural beliefs and practices, practitioners are in a better position to adopt appropriate metaphors and modalities for implementing CBT (e.g., play, art, music) that will prove meaningful to the family (Suzuki et al., 2006).

It is important to establish treatment goals that are valued by the family to improve the working alliance, and cultural practices often influence these goals. If the goals of CBT do not match the goals of the family, parents will be less likely to employ the techniques prescribed by the practitioner. Therefore, it is important for the practitioner to collaborate with the family when establishing goals and ensuring that they are congruent with the family's cultural values and practices. In many cases, it may be necessary to modify traditional goals to ones that are more culturally relevant. Adjusting goals to be more valued by families will give clinicians the opportunity to retain effective CBT strategies while aligning themselves with family members. For example, one of the common targets in treatment for separation anxiety is cosleeping (with the goal of having children sleep alone). This goal may be difficult to address in some families because, while in all cultures children eventually sleep in their own beds, the specific age at which this individuation process is expected to occur may differ (Welles-Nystrom, 2005). Therefore, older children cosleeping with family members can represent common cultural practices and not separation anxiety per se. If families do not feel it is necessary for children to sleep alone in their own beds, the practitioner should work toward applying CBT techniques to help children cope in situations when their parents think it is important for children to be independent (e.g., attending after-school activities without being accompanied by a parent; attending Sunday school with peers while parents are in church). Modifying goals so that they are valued by parents but still relevant to the foci of CBT may enhance treatment acceptability for families with varying cultural norms and values.

Because cultural adaptation can be a critical aspect of effective interventions, practitioners are encouraged to become familiar with the literature on cultural modifications to CBT cited above to develop competence in treating children of all backgrounds who present with anxiety problems.

PHARMACOTHERAPY

Research has established that antidepressant medications like fluvoxamine and sertraline can be efficacious in the treatment of child anxiety disorders (RUPP Anxiety Group, 2001). However, medication is rarely a silver bullet. Often, anxiety symptoms and related impairment can persist even after medications are prescribed and titrated (Pediatric OCD Treatment Study [POTS] Team, 2004). Children with anxiety disorders (with or without comorbid diagnoses) are often so miserable that any form of relief in the short term is humane and appropriate, and a combination of psychosocial and medication interventions may provide the most comprehensive treatment in the short term (Pediatric OCD Treatment Study [POTS] Team, 2004). In our clinical work, we have found that once coping skills are learned and family dynamics are changed, it is often possible to reduce medications and eventually discontinue them, with the close monitoring of the physician and therapist.

SUMMARY: A FAMILY-CONTEXTUAL APPROACH TO CBT FOR CHILDHOOD ANXIETY

CBT is a powerful intervention modality with substantial research support for children with anxiety disorders. Through cognitive therapy techniques, habituation, positive reinforcement, and targeted changes in family communication and boundaries, significant anxiety reduction can be achieved. Including the family in treatment by teaching parenting techniques that promote child autonomy and reduce parental intrusiveness may contribute to treatment gains in at least two ways. First, parents are more likely to play beneficial roles in their children's therapeutic tasks by providing encouragement for independent, courageous behavior, and by reducing unintended contributions to children's avoidant behavior. Second, parents can help children redefine their self-image and develop a sense of confidence and independence that naturally reduces anxiety and promotes courageous behavior. Many practitioners instinctively include parents in treatment due to an underlying philosophy that most disorders are partially rooted in family processes. The Building Confidence program provides a specific rationale and corresponding intervention procedures for family involvement that offer practitioners an efficient and effective means of addressing child anxiety problems in a holistic manner.

PART II

Treatment Manual

CHAPTER FOUR

Building Confidence:
A Family-Based Cognitive-Behavioral
Intervention

• •

In this chapter, the Building Confidence family-based CBT program is presented in full detail. First, general guidelines and parameters of the treatment are described. Then, session-by-session, step-by-step instructions for implementing the program are provided, allowing practitioners to learn the specific evidence-based techniques that were found efficacious in our clinical trial (Wood et al., 2006).

GUIDELINES FOR USING THIS TREATMENT MANUAL

The Building Confidence program is a semistructured treatment for youths with anxiety disorders. This manual provides a plan for each therapy session that includes specific topics, goals, handouts, and homework assignments. The Building Confidence program is designed to be flexibly applied according to the needs of the family. We have organized the sessions in an order that addresses the needs of most families; however, some families benefit from reordering the sessions (also called *modules* to emphasize their self-contained nature). For instance, children who refuse to attend school usually benefit from facing fears (i.e., the exposure therapy module) earlier than Session 8 due to the emergent nature of their anxiety symptoms. As a second example, children who have many friends may not need the optional Playdates module, whereas children who have a focal problem with peer relationships would likely benefit from the Playdates module soon after exposure therapy begins. Finally, some parents may be fairly calm and find it easy to help their children face fears; these parents will require less emphasis on parent emotion management (i.e., the CALM technique in Session 5). Practitioners' judgment about the timing of sessions, the areas of particular emphasis, and the method of presentation is critical in the program, and clinical flexibility is an asset in bringing this treatment to life.

Most sessions include examples of how to describe key concepts to parents or children, which are set off from the text. It is important to note that these examples need to be tailored to the personality and cognitive features of each family seen in treatment. In other words, these examples are intended as general rubrics for presenting CBT concepts in a comprehensible manner for many families, but often require modification to fit each family's cultural, linguistic, emotional, and motivational characteristics (Hwang et al., 2006).

Each session or module has a list of three to five goals. The goals represent the therapeutic material to be covered in a given session. Practitioners should attempt to accomplish each goal during the session. However, the manner of presentation and depth of coverage is flexible—for instance, for a highly verbal child, cartoons might be less appealing, and the use of make-believe stories, play, and role-plays might be a more effective means of psychoeducation. There are many different ways to present therapeutic concepts that can lead to the same acquisition of knowledge, and the therapist must use his or her clinical expertise to determine how best to present information to a particular family. In short, it is important to cover the main goals of each session, but it is not necessary to go point by point through the detailed instructions in each session. These details are provided primarily for therapist education and background, and as a guide to a possible model session rather than as a rigid set of topics to cover in a linear manner.

Flexible Parent and Child Participation in Each Session

Note that the Building Confidence program offers flexibility with regard to the attendees (i.e., parents or children) in each session. Most sessions include three components, which are labeled "With Child Alone (Parents Optional)," "With Parents Alone (Child Optional)," and "With Parents and Child Together." Many factors determine the choices that clinicians will make about whom to ultimately include in the different portions of each session. Factors affecting this decision include available session time, whether the child has clinical needs for private time with the therapist, whether parent-therapist conversations need to be frank and personal and could harm the child's self-esteem or expose the child to upsetting "grown-up" discussions, and the therapist's own preference for a traditional family therapy model (in which the whole family is present for the whole session) versus a more individual therapy model. Generally, including the parents in the child's portion of the session allows for a more economical use of time and makes 50-minute sessions possible. Our research suggests that 60 to 80 minutes are necessary when children are seen alone for a portion of each session, due to the need to repeat topics with children and parents separately. However, the Building Confidence program is often expedited when the parents are seen alone at least briefly because this allows the therapist to give frank advice on how to support challenging homework assignments and gives the parents an opportunity to pose questions or disclose information that could be inappropriate for the child to hear.

Of course, if there is going to be a private parent-therapist portion of a session, it is important for the child to have some sort of supervision in the waiting room and to have an enjoyable activity or homework to do while he or she waits. We have found that 5 to 15 minutes of waiting are tolerable for most school-age children with anxiety disorders.

General Stance of the Therapist

As with any therapy, it is important to establish and maintain rapport with the family throughout the intervention. However, establishing rapport with children with anxiety and their parents is especially important given that children can be slow to warm up, and that they will eventually be asked to face their fears later in treatment—a process made more difficult if trust has not been established first. The first few sessions are used to develop and foster the relationship with the family. As part of this approach, CBT is presented as a collaborative effort in which everyone works together toward an important goal. To coin a therapeutic adage, it is best to offer honey, not vinegar throughout CBT. The therapist is a consultant, not an expert, who provides a friendly, accepting, and supportive environment. It is important to help parents feel that they have not contributed to their child's anxiety, but that they may be able to engage in specialized parenting techniques (that might not be needed with typically developing youths) to assist in the anxiety reduction process. Similarly, children should not feel responsible for or ashamed of their difficulties with anxiety— they are more likely to engage in therapy if they feel that they are not alone in experiencing anxiety, that they are respected, and that they will not be embarrassed during the treatment process.

Helpful Terminology in Working With Families

In the service of maintaining good rapport during child anxiety treatment, it is helpful to use nonstigmatizing, nonclinical language when possible. For example, it can be helpful to refer to CBT as a program rather than as a treatment. The following terms can also be useful to incorporate into the dialogue with families.

- *Building your muscle*—the point of the parenting components of Building Confidence; helping parents become less distressed by their child's behavior and instead focusing on active steps that they can take to help their child face his or her fears
- *Where your child gets stuck*—the point at which the child has been unable to tolerate anxiety in challenging or fearful situations
- *Learning there is nothing to be afraid of*—a primary goal of the program for children vis-à-vis their set of feared (but benign) situations
- *Building the child's confidence*—a primary goal of the program for parents
- *Helpless*—how the child feels due to anxiety problems and poor self-help skills

Building Confidence: An Organizing Principle

A major goal of the Building Confidence program is to build the confidence of each family member. Children with high anxiety often lack self-confidence and may think that they "just can't do it." They may identify with their anxiety and label themselves with anxiety-related terms (e.g., a child with social anxiety might say, "I'm too shy. I just can't handle going someplace with that many kids."). To build confidence, children must (a) learn to face their fears and (b) develop positive roles and activities that are unrelated to anxiety symptoms. Decreasing the negatives (fears) and increasing the positives (e.g., developing self-help skills and friends) simultaneously seems to help many children achieve a qualitative shift in their experience of everyday life, often switching from a gloomy, self-pitying, or grumpy state of mind to a proud, cheerful, and optimistic one.

The program also aims to improve parents' self-confidence. Parents are often unsure about how to respond to their child's anxiety symptoms. CBT assignments can highlight this uncertainty because parents run into difficulties when encouraging their child to face fears, either due to parenting skill deficits or parental emotion regulation problems (i.e., overly sympathetic reactions to their children's anxiety). Parents therefore need to develop the appropriate parenting skills to be an asset to their child. Once these skills have been mastered, parental confidence often begins to increase as well, and the responsibility for setting goals in CBT and following through on them can increasingly shift from the therapist to the parents (a process sometimes referred to as the transfer of control; Silverman & Kurtines, 1996).

Therapist Training

The Building Confidence program is a relatively complex intervention and assumes some prior experience with CBT, child anxiety, and family therapy or parent training. To implement this intervention manual effectively, obtaining appropriate supervision is recommended for the first several cases. Therapists can arrange to receive training and supervision from an experienced practitioner knowledgeable in the use of family CBT for anxiety.

SESSION 1

Intake: Anxiety Assessment

BACKGROUND

In CBT interventions, the client's presenting complaints should be specified clearly right from the beginning. While it is expected that over the course of therapy the client's initial clinical picture will be clarified, it is useful to have an initial impression of the child's particular anxiety-related concerns. This helps the practitioner (1) decide how to approach the child during treatment (e.g., in case separation anxiety or shyness necessitates an adjustment of one's therapeutic style in the early sessions), and (2) provide examples relevant to the child's anxieties right from the start.

GOALS

1. Establish rapport with the family.
2. Obtain parent and child descriptions of current anxiety symptoms.

PREPARATION AND MATERIALS

Obtain copies of relevant child anxiety assessment materials. We recommend using the ADIS-C/P diagnostic interview (Silverman & Albano, 1996) and the MASC (March, 1998) child and parent report forms (see Chapter 1). These can be ordered from the publishers or authors, except for the parent-MASC, which is currently unpublished. It is simply the child report MASC rewritten from the parent's perspective (reporting on the child's anxieties). We have used it extensively in our research (Wood et al., 2002) and found it to be reliable and valid.

Decide how much time to devote to assessment. If you are limited to a 50-minute session and must begin the actual treatment by Session 2, the best strategy is to greet the family, conduct the Separation Anxiety, Social Phobia, and Generalized Anxiety sections of the ADIS-C/P with parent and child together, and use the remaining time to inquire about other relevant possible diagnoses (the ADIS-C/P covers other anxiety disorders such as OCD, depressive disorders, and disruptive behavior disorders). The family may be sent home to fill out the MASC forms.

If you are able to devote 2 hours to the anxiety assessment, it is helpful to conduct the ADIS-C/P separately with the child and parents. This tends to yield a more comprehensive symptom list and allows children to disclose private anxious thoughts or behaviors that parents are unaware of. Parents also feel more comfortable describing the full extent of the child's anxiety symptoms when the child is not with them. While waiting for their family members to be interviewed, parents and children can complete the MASC and additional self-report measures in a waiting room (it is helpful to ask the parents to bring along a babysitter or older sibling to watch over the child in the waiting area during the parent ADIS).

SESSION

Begin by meeting with the family together, welcome them appropriately, and explain the session format for today (e.g., about 50% of the time will be with the child alone and 50% of the time will be with the parents alone). As noted above, the specifics of the session format are flexible and depend on the time available. Point out that the program will last approximately 4 months, and that today the primary goal is to learn about what kinds of difficulties the child has experienced lately (e.g., "What has been going on for your daughter lately?").

Depending on how much time can be devoted to the assessment (50 minutes vs. 2 hours), conduct the diagnostic interview with the family either together or separately (see Preparation and Materials, above). In either case, be sure to focus on the Separation Anxiety, Social Phobia, and Generalized Anxiety sections of the ADIS-C/P first to ensure that the most common anxiety symptom areas are addressed before time runs out. Be sure to follow the guidelines for the administration of the diagnostic interview provided by the authors.

AFTER THE SESSION

It is good clinical practice to write up a brief summary of the child's anxiety symptoms based on the initial diagnostic interview. This helps in later preparing for the development of the fear hierarchy—the all-important treatment plan document that guides exposure therapy (Session 6). Be sure to include the child and parent MASC scores in the brief summary to use as a quantitative baseline measure of the child's initial anxiety level. Mid- and posttreatment MASC scores can then be compared to the baseline scores to assess the degree of anxiety remission. The following is an example of a brief clinical writeup of the ADIS C/P interview.

ADIS-C/P SUMMARY FOR A.B.

A. is an 8-year-old boy of African American descent who appears to be of average height and weight. He presented as a shy, anxious, and timid boy initially, remaining relatively quiet, but was gradually put at ease after playing a short game.

Mr. B. reported that A. complains of stomach pains on the drive to school each morning. The severity of these stomachaches increase as A. approaches school, and A. sometimes cries. A month ago, these behaviors resulted in his missing approximately 1 week of school. Mr. B. mentioned that he had to gradually ease A. back into school after that week of absence. In the past month, A. has been attending school but Mr. B. reports that he must stay with A. most of the school day to ease his anxiety.

Mrs. B. reported that A. becomes upset and tearful, and sometimes cries when she leaves him. A. also often asks her to stay with him. Although A. did not report any worries during his interview, Mrs. B. noted that A. sometimes stays awake until she returns home late at night. A. is often watched by other caregivers such as his grandmother (on mother's side). Although he is comfortable with his grandmother, Mr. and Mrs. B. reported that he is uneasy with new caretakers. Mrs. B. also reported that there are some places that are difficult for him to go without his parents. While A. can play in a room by himself, he prefers to be near his parents and periodically checks (by calling out) to make sure his parents are still there. In addition, Mrs. B. commented that A. is afraid of the dark and requires her to turn on the lights for him before he enters a room. A. does not like to be in the bathroom by himself and asks his mother or father to accompany him. Both A. and Mrs. B. confirm that a strict bedtime routine occurs every night. Mrs. B. will give A. a shower, read to A., and they will fall asleep together in A.'s trundle bed at 8:30 P.M. every night. If A. wakes up in the middle of the night and his mother is not beside him, he calls for her. This regime is fairly new as A. was cosleeping with his parents until about a month ago. Although A. has had sleepovers with his 4-year-old cousin, all of them have occurred in his own house. Mr. and Mrs. B. have asked A. if he wanted to sleep over at his cousin's house, but A. refused and told his parents that he is too shy and scared. Mrs. B. reports that A. would never agree to sleep over at another house unless his mother or father stayed with him.

Mrs. B. notes that A.'s separation anxiety moderately interferes with various areas of his life. Anxious feelings limit him from making new friends in social situations and maintaining bonds with old friends because he is too attached to his parents. Even when other children invite him to play, A. always prefers to be with his parents. In addition, both Mr. and Mrs. B.

report that their freedom is constrained by A.'s need to have them around all the time. Mr. B. reports significant disruptions at his job due to staying with A. during the school day this month. Mrs. B. notes that when it is A.'s bedtime, her day is over too. She has to go to sleep at 8:30 every night to accommodate his anxiety. Mr. and Mrs. B. make consistent compromises in their lives to cater to A.'s fears. Finally, A.'s periodic school refusal and anxiety-related trips to the nurse as well as his lack of independence in the classroom (relying on father's presence) appear to be significant school-related impairments. A. enjoys Lego, Gameboy, T-ball, and drawing.

Child MASC T-score: 68
Parent MASC raw score: 54

Diagnosis: Separation anxiety disorder (severity rating: 5 [on ADIS-C/P 0–8 scale])

SESSION 2

Functional Analysis and Rapport Building

BACKGROUND
The main goals of the second session are to establish rapport with the child and parents and to identify the antecedents, behaviors, and consequences (ABCs) associated with the child's anxiety symptoms, with particular emphasis on parental responses to anxious behavior (which may reinforce the child's anxiety). This analysis of ABCs is often called a *functional analysis of behavior.* As time and opportunity permit, the therapist can begin to screen for parent-child interaction patterns that may contribute to the child's anxiety symptoms. The most common pattern is intrusive, overprotective, or overinvolved parenting (see Chapter 2). The information gathered in this session will guide the formation of a specific treatment plan for the family.

Note that the reward system is very important in eliciting the child's motivation and enthusiasm to participate in session activities and homework. As noted in Chapter 3, rewards are an integral part of effective CBT—but they do not need to be continued for the rest of the child's life, just until the child becomes truly comfortable with the situations he or she fears or avoids.

GOALS
1. Describe the goals of the program to the child and parents.
2. Introduce the idea of anxiety-provoking situations to the child with the cartoon in Figure 4.1.
3. Establish the concepts of "challenges" (homework) and rewards.
4. Learn about the child's typical day.
5. Conduct a functional analysis on one of the child's key anxiety symptoms.

PREPARATION AND MATERIALS

- Prepare (photocopy) parent handouts: Building Confidence Program handout, Parents' Homework handout, Behavior Record Form.
- Prepare (photocopy) child handouts: Challenge 1 handout, Figure 4.1 cartoon.
- Ask the parents to bring favorite toys, games, or books to the session that the child can show the therapist.

SESSION

With Parents and Child Together (10% of the Session)

Meet briefly and explain the format of typical treatment sessions (for example, about 30% of the time with the child alone and about 30% of the time with parents alone, and 40% of the time with both). As noted above, the specifics of the session format are flexible and depend on the time available and the therapist's preference for a traditional family therapy approach (see Flexible Parent and Child Participation in Each Session, on p. 73).

With Child; Parents Optional (About 30% of the Session)

Build rapport.

Engage in an activity or conversation that is of particular interest to the child based on your knowledge about him or her. Activities can include looking at the toy or game that the child brought along, looking around the therapy room, playing a game that the therapist has in the room, or chatting about any topic that may appeal to the child. Make comments expressing interest (e.g., "So I hear that you are playing Little League this year!") or ask questions that are relevant to the child's activities and interests. Let the child know that you will stop engaging in the activity to do some other things in a while, but that you like to make time to have fun when he or she comes to visit.

Briefly orient the child to the program.

Orient the child to the goals of the program. Generally, this should be tailored to concerns that the child has disclosed to the therapist in Session 1. For example, if the child has separation anxiety but emphasized distress about problems with friends, then helping with friends should be highlighted as a goal of the program. Generally, in addition to the child's specific concerns, the therapist should also note that the program entails learning about thoughts and feelings, and knowing how to solve problems.

Introduce the idea of thoughts, feelings, and behaviors related to anxiety with a cartoon.

Use the cartoon in Figure 4.1 to introduce an activity that focuses on the analysis of anxious thoughts, feelings, and behaviors. Using a conversational style, talk with the child about what is going on in the picture. Encourage the child to describe his or her impression of the cartoon without being pushy or didactic. Using a Socratic questioning approach (see Chapter 3), highlight the following points: The child depicted is giving a speech at school; she appears anxious or frightened (this is a good time to assess the child's ability to describe feelings and to adopt his or her specific way of describing anxiety); the reason that she might be anxious is that she might make a mistake and others might laugh (one example of a Socratic question would be, "I wonder what she is worried will go wrong during her speech?"). Encourage the child with praise that is appropriate to his or her temperament (mild for reserved children, bright and cheery for outgoing, active children) for any portion of his or her comments or responses that shows understanding about the situation depicted.

Explain rewards and Challenges.

Explain that each week the child will be assigned a Challenge to complete at home. It is great if children write down their responses on the worksheet. They can ask their parents to help if they would like. A term such as *weekly assignment* can be used as well. Many children are likely to react negatively to the term *homework,* although that is the easiest way to conceptualize these assignments.

Talk with the child about the meaning of the term *challenge.* Point out that challenges are problems that can be "a bit difficult but a bit fun," we learn from them, and we feel proud when we complete them. If the child has disclosed any heroes or favorite characters in the conversation so far, use them to discuss how many people face challenges, and that by overcoming challenges people become stronger, smarter, and sometimes even famous!

> For instance, you know how you really like Luke in *Star Wars*? He faces a lot of challenges, right? What are some of the challenges he faces? . . . Exactly! But, in the end, that's how he beats the emperor and saves the galaxy, right? Challenges are things that take some effort, but usually help us when we overcome them.

A reward system will be set up to encourage the child to do the Challenges. The child will receive a point or sticker (depending on age, gender, maturity) from the therapist for each Challenge completed. Points will add up to small fun rewards or privileges the child will enjoy. "We can talk about the kinds of rewards next time."

Assign a Challenge task of writing about a cartoon depicting anxiety (see Challenge 1). The child is to describe what is going on in the picture, how the character feels, and why she feels that way. Note that this is just like what the child did today with the other cartoon.

With Parents; Child Optional (About 60% of Session)

Review the content of the child's session.

Summarize the child's session briefly. Mention that the child has a short assignment to complete and bring to the next session, and that you will be setting up a reward system to encourage the completion of Challenge assignments and to make the program more fun. The parents should help the child with Challenge 1 if needed and remind him or her to bring the worksheet back at Session 3 to get the point or sticker.

Introduce the purpose of this session.

To provide general information about the program to the parents and collect more specific information about the child to develop an effective treatment plan.

Orient parents to the intervention program.

Give the parents a copy of the Building Confidence Program handout. In addition to covering the points on the handout, emphasize that because they spend many more hours with their child, parents have a great opportunity to help the child use the new skills learned in therapy.

Parents benefit from learning how to help their child employ new coping skills. Dealing with anxiety is difficult, and this program provides parents with the skills and confidence needed to help their child handle tough situations. This point may benefit from a humorous presentation (e.g., "We want to build up your muscle too, so you can handle your child's tantrums and anxiety!").

The program is fairly structured. Each session will have an agenda and follow a plan to help the child cope with anxiety. Some sessions focus on developing techniques aimed at helping the child learn how to cope and think about feared situations differently; some sessions are used for practicing these techniques and applying them to new situations. How quickly the family attains their treatment goals is related to how often the parents and child complete the weekly assigned Challenge tasks.

Ask about a typical day.

> Now I'd like to have you tell me about a typical weekday for your child, starting with the morning routine.

As the parents describe a typical day, identify specific anxious behaviors such as "makes a big fuss every morning to try to avoid going to school," or "won't talk when neighborhood kids come over to play." Parents may focus on a variety of behavioral problems (e.g., fights with siblings), but guide the discussion toward problematic behaviors related to anxiety.

Help the parents focus on two or three daily anxious behaviors. Parents may initially be too general when describing these anxious behaviors (e.g., "He seems worried"). Prompt them to expand on general problems with questions such as, "When does he worry," "What does he worry about," and "What does he do to make you know that he is worried?" On the Behavior Record Form (part of the parent's homework packet), write down these two or three behaviors.

Conduct a functional analysis of behavior (ABCs).

For at least one of the target anxious behaviors (ideally the most salient and distressing for the parents), discuss the problem in depth. It is not necessary to adhere to the following order of questions.

Step 1: Assess specific antecedents of the anxious behavior (e.g., "When do you first notice that your child is anxious?"; "What leads up to the child refusing to go into school?"). What is the main cue that triggers anxiety in the child (e.g., "When the child gets in the car on the way to school, is this when it becomes clear she is anxious?")

After the child's anxiety has become noticeable, what makes it escalate, what factors seem to make the anxiety increase (e.g., driving into the parking lot of the school, the child begins trembling)?

Ask what the parent is thinking and feeling at each stage of the child's anxiety buildup (e.g., when the child is asking many questions, what is the parent thinking and feeling; when the child becomes angry, what is the parent thinking and feeling).

Step 2: Assess the child's behavior when the anxiety reaches its peak (e.g., the child refuses to go into school and starts to cry). Have the parents describe the child's highest level of escalation in detail.

Ask how the parents respond to the child's behavior as it builds up to the peak phase. Has anything been effective or ineffective at getting the child through the feared situation? Does the child act the same with both parents?

Step 3: Assess the consequences of the child's anxious behavior (e.g., "When the child refuses to go into school, what happens?") Does the child face the perceived threat or avoid it? If the child avoids it, how does he or she do so? Does an argument occur between the parents and child (i.e., is the child receiving negative attention)?

What is the parent's emotional reaction once the child's anxiety is reduced? Is the parent relieved, guilty, angry with the child, or frustrated?

Describe the parents' homework assignment briefly.

FIGURE 4-1.

HANDOUT

Challenge 1: What's Going on Here?

FIGURE 4-2.

What is *happening* in this picture?

_____

_____

_____

How does the girl *feel*?

_____

_____

Why does she feel this way? (Hint: think about what she is scared might happen.)

_____

_____

**When you're done, give yourself a pat
on the back for finishing Challenge 1!**

HANDOUT

Building Confidence Program

COGNITIVE-BEHAVIORAL THERAPY FOR CHILDREN

- The first several sessions focus on how to recognize anxiety and other emotions, as well as how to identify anxious thoughts.
- During these initial sessions, children learn strategies to help cope with their anxious feelings and thoughts (e.g., how to use logic to challenge fearful thoughts).
- Later in the program, children are encouraged to face their fears. They slowly attempt more difficult situations, using the new coping skills that they have learned.

THE ROLE OF PARENTS IN THE PROGRAM

- Parents act like coaches by reinforcing lessons that children learn during their sessions and encouraging the children to use their new skills.
- The program teaches parents communication techniques that help children enhance their coping skills.

BENEFITS OF THIS PROGRAM

- Research shows high success rates when children and their parents participate in this program. The main study of the Building Confidence program found that 79% of the children did not have an anxiety disorder after treatment.
- Because parents learn key principles of anxiety management, they can help their children continue to face their fears even after the program is over.

HANDOUT

Parent's Homework

BUILDING CONFIDENCE PROGRAM—SESSION 2

Track your child's behavior! Use the Behavior Record Form and fill in two or three of your child's typical anxious behaviors. This week, record whether your child engages in these behaviors each day and how you respond. This form is intended to help you and the therapist identify what is leading to and helping with your child's anxiety problems.

**Remember to bring the Behavior Record Form
to the next session!**

Behavior Record Form

Directions: Each day, record your child's anxious behavior and your response.

I am tracking these two or three behaviors:

_____   _____   _____

Example:

Behavior: My child refused to get out of the car and go into school by himself.

My response: I said I could tell he was nervous about leaving this morning and I waited.

Child's reaction: After several minutes of waiting, he grumbled and walked into school.

Date	Anxious Behavior	My Response to My Child	My Child's Reaction

SESSION 3

KICK Plan: K Step, **Know** *When You're Nervous*

BACKGROUND

Children with elevated anxiety have high levels of negative emotion as well as irrational thoughts (see Chapter 1). They need to learn to identify both feelings and thoughts as a first step of coping with anxiety. KICK is an acronym intended to remind children of specific coping methods. The first step, K, is presented in Session 3. Note that the goal of the K step— Knowing I'm Nervous—is to help children become familiar with their own internal cues that signify that they are anxious. Children must be aware that they are experiencing anxiety in a situation if they are to cope effectively with it.

On the basis of the information gathered in Sessions 1 and 2, a treatment plan is presented to the parents in Session 3. Initially, to help parents understand the rationale for the treatment plan, information about the nature of child anxiety (psychoeducation) is presented. A connection between child "misbehavior" and anxiety is emphasized. It is important for the parents to see this connection to help reduce blame, hostility, and other kinds of tension between the parents and the child that may have arisen because of the child's coping responses to anxiety (i.e., tantrums, avoidance). Then, based on the functional analysis obtained in Session 2, a treatment plan is presented that is tailored to the specific needs of the family.

GOALS

1. Continue to develop rapport.
2. Review Challenge homework with the child and parents.

3. Teach the family how to identify physiological cues of anxiety (K step).
4. Present a personalized treatment plan to the parents.
5. Assign Challenge homework to the child.

PREPARATION AND MATERIALS

- Prepare a simple reward chart out of colorful paper with a title such as "Jimmy's Smart Chart." Make a column of four sessions (sessions 3–6) and leave space to either write in points or place stickers.
- Photocopy the following handouts: Common Patterns of Child Anxiety, Building Confidence, Challenge 2, and the cartoons in Figures 4.3–4.15 (these will be used in the next few sessions).
- Bring two pages of blank paper, a pencil, and crayons.

SESSION

With Child; Parents Optional (About 40% of the Session)

Build rapport.

For a minute or two, build rapport with the child by chatting about activities or topics of interest to him or her.

Review the Challenge task.

Review the child's Challenge task. If he or she did not write answers on the worksheet, allow the child to complete it verbally by reporting answers in the session. Give gentle corrective feedback to clarify any misinterpretations of the situation. For example, "Oh, so she feels like sitting down? Is that because she feels nervous about giving a speech? Okay—so she feels nervous." Introduce the reward chart with appropriate affective tone (matching the child's personality style, as noted in Session 2). Record appropriate points or stickers on the reward chart. Reemphasize to the child how important the Challenge tasks are, and how the reward chart will lead to something fun for the child.

Identify emotions.

Use cartoons of children depicted in four mood states (Figure 4.3) and work with the child to identify feelings based on expressions and posture.

> Let's look at these cartoons. We're going to play detective and figure out what these people are feeling. See this guy here? I think that he is [*pause*] happy! Know how I can tell? He has a big smile on his face! Do you want to take a turn? What do you think this person is feeling in this picture? Is there anything about her face that gives up clues about what she is feeling?

Use Socratic questions (see Chapter 3, Emotion Education, Identifying Maladaptive Schemata, and Cognitive Restructuring) as necessary to help the child identify the emotion and pick out facial and body cues that inform us about the emotion each character is feeling. The chart below is primarily for the therapist's reference and identifies some key bodily and facial features of the basic emotions. Children do not need to learn or identify every feature of each emotion—the main point is that distinctions can be made among the emotions based on the way someone looks.

> What about the face, in particular, tells us that he is feeling sad? Is there something about his mouth that gives us clues? What about his eyes? They have tears? Okay, so let's review—what are the main ways we can tell that someone is sad from looking at their face?

97

Emotion	Cues
Fear (scared, nervous, afraid, anxious)	Wide eyes; sometimes a frown; sometimes an open mouth; raised eyebrows; shivering; sweating
Anger	Squinting; angled eyebrows; furrowed brow (wrinkled forehead); pursed lips; red face
Sadness	Crying; frown; drooping shoulders; slumped over (head in hands); looking away from others
Happiness	Smile/grin; laughing; wrinkles on the sides of eyes

Do this for the four basic emotions. Some children will want to distinguish between surprise and fear (the former usually includes a gaping-mouth). Others will want to add more complex emotions such as jealousy—allow them to do so to encourage rapport, but ensure that they understand the key features of anxiety.

Help the child understand that when it comes to fear, there are different words for the same feeling: feeling afraid, scared, nervous, or anxious. They all mean roughly the same thing. Ask which word the child uses and likes best. Be sure to use this word in the future in discussing fear and anxiety.

Know when you're nervous: The K step.

Disclose a situation that causes the therapist modest anxiety that is socially acceptable such as going on roller coasters or giving speeches (give examples common among most children and avoid examples that might model new anxious thoughts for the child). Use appropriate affect to engage and maintain the child's interest and attention. Describe the physiological cues that the situation elicits (e.g., racing heart, trembling, sweating, fast breathing, stomachache, light-headedness, headache, aches and pains—it is often best if these physiological cues match some of the child's known somatic expressions of anxiety).

☛ **Therapist Note:** The therapist's use of modeling (disclosing fears) allows the child to witness a skill being used—in this case, appropriate identification of anxious feelings. Modeling helps the child learn how to use skills and normalizes the experience of anxiety.

If the child volunteers a feared situation during or after this disclosure, help him or her brainstorm on the kinds of physiological reactions he or she had. Otherwise, return to the cartoons in Figures 4.4–4.15 and select examples that show clear physiological reactions to fear that can be portrayed in a picture (trembling, sweating, stomachache). Ask what the cartoon child's body is doing that portrays anxiety. Ask rhetorically,

Is that one way we could tell the child is afraid? Yes, the way our body feels is one way we can tell if we're afraid.

Introduce the concept of using physiological cues as a signal that one is becoming anxious.

Before we know what to do about anxiety, we have to know when we're becoming anxious. We refer to this as the K step: Knowing I'm Nervous. *K* stands for Knowing!

Write down KICK vertically on a blank piece of paper. Fill in the K step, Knowing I'm Nervous.

We're going to be learning the KICK plan as a way to feel better when we become afraid. That's what this program is about. And we just learned the first step, K!

Say (while drawing an "inverted U" mountain and a stick figure "kid" on a blank piece of paper):

> Let's practice: Let's say a kid didn't like going up to high places. And then she had to go to the top of a mountain and look down. Then she started shivering and sweating. Her eyes got really wide open. [*Quickly draw squiggles and circles to represent shivers, sweat, and wide eyes.*] How do you think she is feeling? How can you tell? Why not happy? Why not sad?

If the child is still engaged, ask if he or she can think of something that would make "most kids" afraid. Ask the child to make up a story (offer to draw a stick figure of the story or, if the child would like to do so, offer her or him the pencil or crayons) about a child who was in this situation. Ask how people could tell the child was afraid by looking at him or her. If needed, use Socratic questioning (see Chapter 3) to help the child explain this.

Tip: These exercises may need to be repeated in later sessions to ensure that they are mastered.

Challenge task.

Assign the child Challenge 2. The child is to list the facial and bodily cues in the cartoon that could reflect anxiety.

With Parents and Child Together (10% of the Session)

Setting up an initial reward.

Inform the parents that the child is to complete a new Challenge task at home, and may or may not need help with it.

Discuss small rewards the child might earn for doing four Challenges (e.g., four points or stickers). The therapist may provide the first reward, or the parents can do so. Make suggestions of privileges or small treats or trinkets (e.g., staying up 15 minutes late, getting to chose a favorite dinner or other food, getting a pack of trading cards). Whatever is chosen, the parent has to endorse it and the child has to want it, if it is to be an effective motivator. Note that rewards will be discussed more fully in later sessions—this is just a start.

☞ **Therapist Note:** Rewards are not optional in CBT. Parents should be aware that rewards are short term but necessary for this kind of program to teach children skills that they need—to keep them motivated.

With Parents; Child Optional (About 50% of the Session)

Inquire about the parents' completion of homework.

Briefly inspect the Behavior Record Form and inform the parents that their responses are useful and help illustrate how the child's anxiety manifests at home.

Discuss the nature and causes of anxiety.

If the parents were not present for the meeting with the child, focus on explaining the K step briefly. Use several of the cartoons to explain how this concept was taught to the child. Emphasize the facial and physiological cues associated with anxiety, and how this lets children and others know that they have become anxious.

Briefly cover the causes of anxiety (see Chapter 2), focusing mainly on genetic factors and early personality traits. Avoid parent blaming but acknowledge that parents can play a role in helping the child overcome anxiety by using special parenting techniques.

Also emphasize that (a) anxiety is experienced by everyone, and is only a problem when it interferes with important areas of life (e.g., school, making friends, or getting along with the family), and (b) because it is an expectable reaction to some situations, the aim is not to completely eliminate anxiety, but simply to reduce its intensity and help the child cope better with it.

Discuss the child's pattern of anxiety.

Present the Common Patterns of Child Anxiety handout to the parents. With input from the parents and knowledge from the Session 2 interview, fill in the blanks for the ways that the child manifests anxiety during one of the child's most salient anxious situations, and what he or she does to reduce anxiety and regulate emotions (seeking help or avoiding). It is generally easiest to choose the behavior discussed in the functional analysis in Session 2.

Describe the treatment plan, personalized to the family.

Present the Building Confidence handout to the parents. Use relevant information about the child and parents to help personalize the presentation.

> Anxiety makes many children feel helpless and frightened in certain situations. They lose confidence in themselves and their abilities.
>
> For instance, you mentioned last week that Andy believes that he just doesn't know what to say when he is meeting new kids. He has lost confidence in his social skills. Building his confidence is the primary goal of this program.
>
> In this program, children learn coping skills like problem solving that can help them manage their emotions. With children, I refer to this as the KICK plan.
>
> A very important part of the program is helping Andy to gradually face his fears. This will help him feel more confident and in control of his anxiety.

For instance, Andy is scared to sleep by himself. After he learns how to problem solve and calm himself down, we are going to make a plan with him to slowly try out sleeping alone for longer and longer periods of time, so that he can practice using his coping skills and build confidence without being rushed to do it all at once.

I will spend a portion of each session teaching you skills that will help when Andy is feeling anxious. Children often do not know what they are feeling. Parents can help children identify their feelings and can help them learn when to use their coping skills.

An important step in Building Confidence is to help the child find new roles and a different way of looking at himself.

For instance, Andy has lost some friends recently because he refuses to go on playdates. We are going to work with both of you to help him restore those friendships or begin some new ones, so that he can enjoy one of the great experiences of childhood, having close friends. You also mentioned that Andy has been depending on you for some things, like getting dressed, that many 10-year-olds do for themselves. We'll help him become more independent with that so he can begin to feel more mature. These kinds of new roles will build up his confidence.

Warn the parents that they should not expect to see improvement in the child's anxiety during the first phase of treatment.

The first phase of the program (the first seven sessions) is focused on teaching the child and the parents skills that will help the child learn to manage anxiety more effectively. However, until the child actually begins to face his or her fears in the second half of the program (i.e., starting with Session 8), he or she is unlikely to exhibit observable improvement.

FIGURE 4-3.

FIGURE 4-4.

FIGURE 4-5.

FIGURE 4-6.

FIGURE 4-7.

FIGURE 4-8.

FIGURE 4-9.

FIGURE 4-10.

FIGURE 4-11.

FIGURE 4-12.

FIGURE 4-13.

FIGURE 4-14.

FIGURE 4-15.

HANDOUT

Challenge 2: Can You Tell What I'm Feeling?

FIGURE 4-16.

How does this boy *feel*?

_____

List five things you noticed that tell you how he is feeling.

1. _____

2. _____

3. _____

4. _____

5. _____

**When you're done, give yourself a pat
on the back for finishing Challenge 2!**

Common Patterns of Child Anxiety

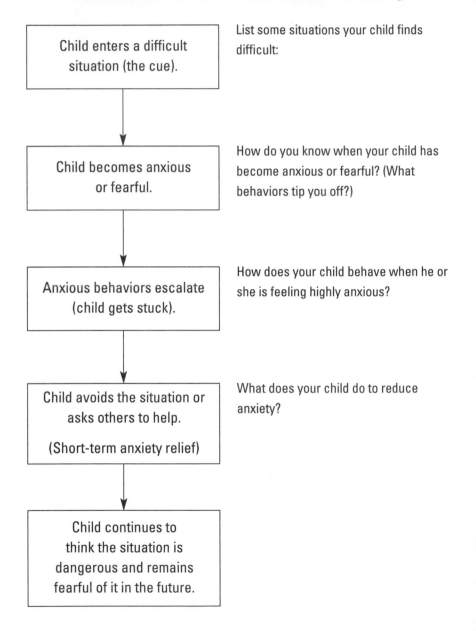

Child enters a difficult situation (the cue).	List some situations your child finds difficult:
Child becomes anxious or fearful.	How do you know when your child has become anxious or fearful? (What behaviors tip you off?)
Anxious behaviors escalate (child gets stuck).	How does your child behave when he or she is feeling highly anxious?
Child avoids the situation or asks others to help. (Short-term anxiety relief)	What does your child do to reduce anxiety?
Child continues to think the situation is dangerous and remains fearful of it in the future.	

Building Confidence

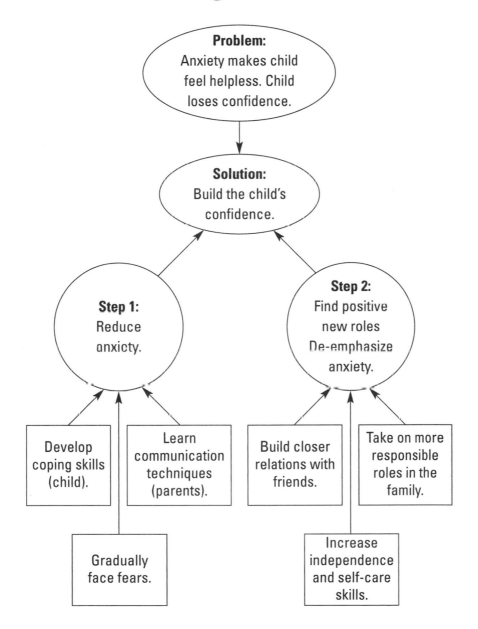

SESSION 4

KICK Plan: I Step, **Identify** *Icky Thoughts and Encourage Independence*

BACKGROUND

The second step of the KICK plan, I—Identify Icky Thoughts—is presented in Session 4. The rationale for the I step is described in Chapter 3 (Addressing Maladaptive Schemata); irrational thoughts are a core aspect of clinical anxiety that must be identified to employ cognitive restructuring (which is taught in Session 5).

This is the first session in which parental intrusiveness and autonomy granting are addressed directly. From a structural family therapy perspective, this session introduces a key avenue for improving parent-child boundaries without alienating the family. By encouraging children to engage in private self-help tasks independently, therapists can effectively intervene with an enmeshed parent-child coalition that is keeping the child in an immature or excessively mature role with one or both parents. Parents are treated as collaborators rather than barriers in this session's focus on self-help skills, and because of this nonblaming approach, parents soon begin to recognize on their own other aspects of parent-child enmeshment and intrusiveness that would benefit from change (e.g., excessive physical affection). By teaching parents the importance of children's autonomy in the treatment of anxiety and by offering them concrete parenting skills and assignments that provide them a sense of control and empowerment, parents who may have previously enjoyed a dependent parent-child relationship can become equally strong advocates for children's independence. It is critical to emphasize that children develop self-confidence when they are able to do activities that other children their age can do with regard to self-help skills, and that it enhances self-esteem to think of oneself as, for instance, a normal 10-year-old. Children will, in turn, feel more confident and courageous.

GOALS

1. Review Challenge homework with the child and parents.
2. Exemplify the connection between anxious thoughts and anxious feelings (I step).
3. Explain the importance of independence and plan three self-help skills for the child to work on.
4. Teach parents two communication skills: respecting a child's struggle and giving choices.
5. Assign Challenge homework to the child and parents.

PREPARATION AND MATERIALS

- The therapist and parents may find Chapter 2 from *How to Talk So Kids Will Listen and Listen So Kids Will Talk* (Faber & Maslich, 2001) helpful as background reading on the importance of developing independence in children and how parents can help.
- Photocopy the following handouts: Challenge 3, Self-Help Skills, Five Tips to Help With Self-Care Skills, Encouraging Independence—How Parents Can Help, Parents' Homework, Self-Help Skills Diary
- Bring the photocopied cartoons in Figures 4.3–4.15, including those that were used in Session 3.
- Bring the inverted U mountain drawing, partially completed KICK plan sheet, and rewards chart used in Session 3.
- Bring two pages of blank paper, pencil, and crayons.

SESSION

With Child; Parents Optional (About 35% of the Session)

Build rapport.

For a minute or two, build rapport with the child by chatting about activities or topics of interest to him or her.

Review the Challenge task.

Review the child's Challenge task. If he or she did not write down responses on the worksheet, allow the child to complete it with you. Give gentle corrective feedback to clarify any misinterpretations. Record appropriate points or stickers on the reward chart. Praise the child's effort.

Explain the I step.

Return to the cartoons used in Session 3. Discuss the kinds of thoughts that each character may be having. Begin with an example to allow for modeling:

> Okay, let's have a look at this cartoon again. We're going to play detective again—figuring out this time what some of these kids are thinking about. Okay, I'll go first. . . . Let's see. He's standing beside a swimming pool, and we already know he *feels* afraid because we saw he was shivering and sweating. So, I think he might be thinking: "If I go into the pool, I might sink to the bottom because I'm not a good swimmer!" Do you think that's what he's saying to himself?

Negotiate with the child to come up with a reasonable thought that reflects anxiety in the situation. Once a thought is agreed upon, draw a thought bubble over the cartoon child's head and write in the thought. While writing the thought, say it again out loud with affect to keep the child's attention. The child may do the writing, too.

Try a second, third, and even fourth cartoon depending on the child's willingness and interest. Include the inverted U-shaped mountain drawing if the child enjoyed it in Session 3. The child can draw his or her own cartoons, too. Use Socratic questions to transfer the work of developing appropriate anxious thoughts for each cartoon to the child. However, do so slowly to evaluate the child's grasp of the concept. If he or she is developing thoughts that do not reflect anxiety, ignore the incorrect response and ask a Socratic question to lead the child to the right response:

> Oh, well, do you think that she is also afraid about messing up in her speech? What might happen if she said something wrong when giving the speech? What might the other kids do?

If the child provides a response in third-person language, transform the thought into first-person language for the child and check in to see if this is what the child had in mind (e.g., for "They'd laugh at her," the therapist can respond, "So, she might say to herself, 'I'm afraid they'll laugh at me?'") Write the correctly worded thought in the thought bubble while saying it out loud to help model and reinforce the use of thought language in the first person for this exercise. Continue with cartoon examples to build up the child's level of mastery.

Disclose anxious thoughts that were experienced in the therapist's example provided in Session 3 for the K step. For example, for a fear of roller coasters:

> So remember how I said I get nervous about roller coasters? Well, do you know what kind of thoughts I had when I once went on a roller coaster? I thought, "Oh boy, I'm afraid the cart is going to fly off the track and I'll get really hurt!"

If the child volunteers a feared situation during or after this disclosure, help the child or her brainstorm on the kinds of thoughts he or she had. Some children enjoy sketching the situation out as a cartoon and adding a thought bubble for the icky thought.

Explain the I step—it is important to identify icky or irritating thoughts, so that we know what is bothering us when we are afraid. The specific term used depends on the child's maturity level and personality; it is easiest to simply ask whether he or she prefers *icky* or *irritating.*

Write the I step on the KICK plan sheet: Icky (or Irritating) Thoughts.

Review the first two steps of the KICK plan.

Okay, in a minute we're going to tell your mom about the KICK plan. First, let's try to remember what each step is. Okay, the K step was [pause] that's right, Knowing I'm Nervous, and we use that step to figure out when our body is feeling nervous. What kinds of things do our bodies do to tell us we're afraid? Okay, now the I step was [pause] right, Icky Thoughts. Can you give me an example of the kinds of thoughts kids get when they go someplace scary, like a new roller coaster? [pause] Great. Okay, we're almost ready to tell your mom all about it!

Challenge task.

Assign the child Challenge 3. It corresponds to the K and I steps of the KICK plan, and is intended to help the child contemplate the anxious thoughts that the character in the cartoon might be experiencing.

With Parents; Child Optional (About 40% of Session)

Introduce the concept of encouraging independence.

Explain that an important role that parents can play in addressing their child's anxiety problems involves helping the child to become more independent. Remind the parents that children can build their self-confidence by developing new roles, as discussed in Session 3—becoming more independent makes children feel mature and confident.

Emphasize the importance of helping children develop self-help skills.

Initiate a conversation about the value of developing independence in self-help skills: (a) This is an important area of functioning that is often impaired in children with anxiety, who tend to be less independent than their peers, and (b) developing more independence in self-help skills gives children a sense of personal control—we have found this to be very important for improving children's anxiety problems.

Personalize this point for the family by referring to specific self-help behaviors that the child does not typically perform, based on parent report or personal observations:

> Anxiety often interferes with self-help skills in children, such as choosing clothes or grooming independently [choose relevant examples]. Many children with anxiety are behind their friends in these areas, and they can end up feeling immature. We have found that it can be very helpful for parents to encourage their children to engage in these tasks without help. Over the course of our program, we've seen this lead to increases in self-confidence and more courageous behavior in many children.

Identify three self-help skills to target.

Present the Self-Help Skills worksheet to the parents. Propose that this week the child should be encouraged to engage in three age-appropriate self-help skills that he or she does not normally perform independently (i.e., needs a parent's help with). Encourage the parents to review the list of examples on the Self-Help Skills worksheet.

☞ **Therapist Note:** It is important to distinguish between what the child is capable of doing and what he or she actually does. Many parents state that their child is capable of certain behaviors (e.g., independent bathing), but when questioned further, the parents acknowledge that in practice they still assist with part of the task (e.g., helping the child out of the bath or washing hair). Priority should be given to the more private self-help skills, if relevant (e.g., dressing or bathing).

When selecting the three skills, try to choose "low-hanging fruit"—activities that the child could easily do alone but is just not doing independently at the moment. Always ask thoroughly about the skills at the top of the list, because many children with anxiety are not entirely independent with them even though they could be.

Review the five tips on the worksheet with the parents. These strategies help ensure the greatest chance of success for the homework assignment.

Prepare parents for the possibility that children may resist new self-help skills.

Children may resist changes in the daily routine, especially if they perceive doing self-help skills as a chore. The goal is to have the child do the tasks without providing help, even if the child struggles. Suggest that there are two useful ways of responding to problems that arise as the child tries to perform these tasks: showing respect for a child's struggle and giving choices (Faber & Maslich, 2001).

Pass out the Encouraging Independence handout. Note that "respecting a child's struggle" helps children master new skills—it involves waiting patiently and giving children time to figure out their own solutions to tasks such as how to do daily self-care skills.

With respect to giving choices, the choices do not always have to be significantly different from each other—it is the feeling of having a choice that helps (e.g., "Do you want to wait 1 minute before starting your bath, or would you prefer 2 minutes?"). Discuss how even small choices give children a sense of control that can be very helpful.

Troubleshoot the self-help skills task with the parents.

Have the parents describe what they imagine their child would do and say if he or she was resistant or having difficulty with the tasks. Take the role of the parent in responding to the child in these situations, using the skills from the Encouraging Independence handout. Then, switch roles.

Plan for the conversation with the child.

Mention to the parents that an important part of starting the child on new self-help skills is initially presenting the idea in a positive manner. Plan on how to introduce the idea to the child when he or she joins the therapist and family at the end of the session. Present the Parents' Homework assignment.

☛ **Therapist Note:** It is generally advisable for the therapist, rather than the parents, to explain the purpose of this task to the child. However, it is important for the parents to own some of the responsibility for suggesting that the child work on the three specific self-help skills by having them describe these tasks to the child during the family meeting.

With Parents and Child Together (25% of the Session)

Review the I step, Challenge task, and points.

- Ask the child to briefly explain the I step to the parents. If the child agrees, use some of the cartoons to give examples

128

of various kinds of thought bubbles that illustrate anxious thoughts.

- Inform the parents that the child is to complete a new Challenge task at home and may or may not need help with it.
- Mention that the child earned another point or sticker toward the first reward (if true).

Briefly explain the reason for the self-help skills assignment to the child.

> Your parents and I were just thinking about things to work on at home this week. Remember how we were talking about learning to do some things by yourself in this program? You know, like learning how to calm yourself down without anyone's help when you're nervous? I also wanted to see if we could talk about making a plan to do some other things by yourself this week. Your parents had some ideas about some things that they thought you would do a good job on without any help.

Encourage the parents to explain the three targeted self-help skills to the child.

Encourage the family to plan on how the child will engage in the self-help skills.

Troubleshoot with the family if the child does not feel comfortable doing the three tasks independently. If the child cannot perform a skill without help, encourage the family to provide a reduced level of help this week on this skill, with the goal of making the child independent eventually. If the child is highly resistant to a task, switch to an easier task for now. Write the agreed-upon three tasks on the Self-Help Skills handout.

Challenge 3: Guess What I'm Thinking

FIGURE 4-17.

How does this girl *feel*?

_____

List two things that you noticed about her face that tell you how she is feeling.

1. _____
2. _____

This girl has some *icky* (or *irritating*) thoughts. Imagine what she is thinking about. What is she scared will happen?

_____

_____

_____

_____

HANDOUT

Self-Help Skills

Think of three daily self-help tasks that your child could do independently. Here are some tasks that other parents have successfully worked on with their children:

Age Norm	Skill
6+	Choosing own clothes and dressing self
6+	Tying shoes
7+	Taking a bath independently
7+	Brushing teeth or combing hair without help
8+	Putting own dirty clothes into hamper
9+	Making breakfast or a bag lunch
9+	Putting own homework into backpack
10+	Having a small choice about bedtime or bedtime routine
11+	Getting up in the morning without a reminder (using an alarm)
11+	Being responsible for own bedroom (neatness, decorations)
11+	Having some input on the order of the after-school schedule

The tasks should have to do with care of self and one's own space or activities, not family chores like washing dishes or doing yard work.

The skills we will work on this week are:

1. _____
2. _____
3. _____

See "Five Tips to Help With Self-Care Skills"

Five Tips to Help With Self-Care Skills

Children who are used to getting help with self-care skills will need to learn how to perform these tasks independently. Talk with your child about it this week. Here are some tips:

1. Point out that it's really important for kids to learn to do some things for themselves—it can make them feel more grown-up. It can help to say that you've been helping your child do some things that he or she could probably do alone.

2. Consider finding a small reward that the child might want to work for. For instance, if a child is able to start a bath and wash her hair by herself, she may watch 15 minutes of TV after the bath before going to bed.

3. Most important, once the child agrees to do the self-help tasks, do not help him or her do it. Respect the child's struggle and allow him or her to try and fail and try again. It is fine to provide occasional reminders at first. But try not to do the task for the child.

4. If your child is having a hard time with a task, help him or her become independent by slowly reducing the amount of help you are giving.

5. Give your child a casual but descriptive compliment each time he or she does a self-help task successfully. "Your hair smells nice. I can tell you used your favorite shampoo!"

Encouraging Independence—
How Parents Can Help

Children with anxiety often have low self-confidence. They may rely on others for help with tasks that they could actually do by themselves. It helps children to become more independent and learn that they can do a fine job on their own. There are two principles for encouraging independence in children:

1. **Show respect for the child's struggle.** Children learn by trying, failing, and trying again. Rather than doing their tasks for them, it helps to stay calm and show children that it is okay not to be perfect. You can say: "That can be very hard!" or "You're trying your best!"

   You can also give information that children may not have. "When you button your shirt, it helps to start with the top button." When you hang back, it gives children room to try again (and again, if necessary).

2. **Give choices.** Giving children several choices about how to do a task can make them more willing to try. For instance, with a child trying to make a bag lunch you might ask, "Well, do you think you want peanut butter or tuna today?"

   Choices can help when children are anxious, too. For instance, if a child is feeling shy at a birthday party and asks to be taken home early, you might say, "We're going to stay, but you could always watch the girls play on that computer over there, or we could ask if you could join in the treasure hunt. It's up to you."

   Be positive and firm about the choices. If your child thinks of a good alternative choice, that is fine, too! If your child will not make a decision, it is best to wait it out patiently and stay calm. If you are patient, most children will eventually make a choice.

Parent's Homework

ENCOURAGING INDEPENDENCE

Have your child practice three self-help skills. Each day, record on the Self-Help Skills Diary any new self-help tasks that your child tried and how he or she reacted.

Remember to bring the Self-Help Skills Diary to the next session!

Self-Help Skills Diary

Directions: Each day, encourage your child to do the three self-help routines. Record how it goes on this form.

Example:

Behavior: I encouraged my child to tie shoes by herself.

My child's reaction: She tied them, but she forgot to tie a double loop. She showed me proudly.

My response: I praised her. I did not say anything about the double loop.

Date	I Encouraged My Child to Do This Self-Help Skill	My Child's Reaction	My Response to My Child

SESSION 5

KICK Plan: C Step, Calm *Your Thoughts*

BACKGROUND

As noted in Chapter 3, cognitive restructuring is a CBT technique that involves learning how to evaluate and Challenge irrational thoughts that contribute to feeling anxious. Cognitive restructuring—exemplified by the C step of the KICK plan (Calm Thoughts)—can bolster a child's confidence to face feared situations. By itself this technique generally cannot overcome child anxiety disorders, but when used to develop the courage to test out frightening situations, it can be an invaluable skill. Learning to evaluate the veracity of anxious thoughts may potentially help children avoid developing new irrational fears in the first place.

Strategic family therapy techniques largely composed of parental communication skills are introduced in this session to help improve interactions around the child's anxieties. Some children with anxiety disorders may become irritable or oppositional in anxiety-provoking situations, while others become reserved and aloof. Both of these response patterns can sometimes help the child avoid feared situations. Parents often fail to recognize that these behaviors represent immature attempts to escape situations that children perceive as difficult. Instead, parents may become angry or counter the child's behavior with negative behavior of their own (e.g., arguing, criticizing). However, children benefit more from a calm response to their negative feelings because once these feelings are understood and accepted, children can concentrate more on using effective coping skills, such as the KICK plan.

GOALS

1. Review Challenge homework with the child and parents.
2. Present the C step of the KICK plan.
3. Teach parents the CALM strategy.
4. Teach parents the principle of selective attention.
5. Assign Challenge homework to the child.

PREPARATION AND MATERIALS

- The therapist and parents may find Chapter 1 of *How to Talk So Kids Will Listen and Listen So Kids Will Talk* (Faber & Maslich, 2001) helpful as background reading on the importance of accepting negative feelings.
- Photocopy the following handouts: Challenge 4, CALM, Selective Attention.
- Bring the cartoons in Figures 4.3–4.15, including those that were used in Sessions 3 and 4.
- Bring the inverted U mountain drawing, partially completed KICK plan sheet, and rewards chart used in Sessions 3 and 4.
- Bring two pages blank paper, pencils or pens of several colors, and crayons.

SESSION

With Child; Parents Optional (About 40% of the Session)

Build rapport.

For a minute or two, build rapport with the child by chatting about activities or topics of interest to him or her.

Review the Challenge task.

Review the child's Challenge task. If he or she did not write down responses on the worksheet, allow the child to complete it with you. Give gentle corrective feedback to clarify any misinterpretations. Record appropriate points or stickers on the reward chart. Praise the child's effort and remind him or her that with four points or stickers, the child will earn the agreed-upon reward.

Introduce the C step.

Review the KICK plan sheet briefly. Ask whether the child can recall the first two steps:

Remember what K and I stand for in the KICK plan? . . . Guess what, today we're going to learn what C stands for!

Return to the cartoons used in Sessions 3 and 4. Choose the most favored or salient cartoon to begin with. Review the kinds of feelings and thoughts that the cartoon child may have experienced.

Okay, let's have a look at this cartoon again. Let's try to remember, what was this boy feeling? How could we tell? Yes, his eyes are wide open, so he's probably afraid. Also, he is shaking, remember? When people shake, that is one way we know they are afraid. And remember what kinds of icky thoughts he had? Yes, we wrote them down—he's afraid he's going to sink to the bottom of the pool!

Using the same cartoon, explain that the goal today is to help the cartoon character think of calm thoughts that will help him or her feel better. Begin with an example before asking the child to generate positive thoughts.

For instance, could he say to himself, "I've taken a lot of swimming lessons and my mom says I am a good swimmer. So I don't think that I'll sink if I go in the pool."

Assess the child's initial reactions: "Do you think that saying this would help him feel better?" If the child shows signs of understanding, consider asking if there is another thing the cartoon child could say that could also make him or her feel better. If the child provides an incorrect response, gently provide corrective information without stating that the child is wrong. On the cartoon, write in the positive thought in a thought bubble, next to the original icky thought bubble. Often this is best accomplished using a different colored pencil or pen for calm thoughts (versus icky ones).

Proceed to additional cartoons.

> We're going to play detective again—this time we will figure out what these kids can say to themselves to feel calmer. You know, calm thoughts they can have.

Prompt the child to reidentify the cartoon child's feelings and fearful thoughts. Then negotiate with the child to come up with a reasonable calm thought that could reduce anxiety in the situation. Once this has been agreed upon, draw a thought bubble over the cartoon child's head and quickly write in the thought while saying it again out loud with affect (to keep the child's attention). The child may do the writing, too. It is also fine for the child to draw his or her own cartoons of fearful situations and add thought bubbles.

Use Socratic questions as needed to transfer the work of developing appropriate calm thoughts to the child. However, do so slowly to evaluate the child's grasp of the concept. If he or she is developing thoughts that have little to do with the problem, ignore the incorrect response and ask a Socratic question to lead the child to the right response:

> Okay, how likely is it that the roller coaster cart would fly off the track? Have you ever seen that happen? Me neither! How could she remind herself that she's never actually heard of a roller coaster cart flying off? What could she say to herself? What would her calm thought be? Something like, "I've never heard. . . ."

Allow the child child to finish the sentence if possible.

If the child provides a response in third-person language, transform the thought into first-person language and check in to see if this is what the child had in mind (e.g., for "She has never messed up a speech before," the therapist could say, "So, she might say to herself, 'I have never messed up a speech before?'"). Again, write the correctly worded thought in the thought bubble while saying it out loud to help model and reinforce the use of thought language in the first person for this exercise. This will help the child acquire the skill of cognitive restructuring (which naturally involves first-person thinking). Continue with cartoon examples to build up the child's level of mastery.

As the cartoon exercises go along, weave in two points:

1. The C step in the KICK plan is Calm Your Thoughts. Write this down on the KICK sheet. Explain that all the positive thoughts developed for the cartoon characters are calm thoughts—thoughts that can make the child feel calm and not anxious. If the child's maturity level is sufficient, directly draw this link: "Our thoughts can change our feelings."

2. There are two types of calm thoughts that are often especially helpful: (a) How likely is the bad thing to happen, and (b) if it did happen, so what? Sometimes one of these types of calm thoughts is more useful than the other. The first question can make children feel better when they know that something almost never happens (e.g., the child's mother getting in a horrible car accident on the way to work—"It's never happened before, right? How likely is it to happen now?"). The second question is more appropriate when children think something "a little bad" could happen, but that it would not be the end of the world (e.g., making a mistake during a speech—"Sometimes I ask

myself when I worry about this: 'If I mess up nobody will notice, so does it really matter? Probably not, right?'").

Return to the therapist's example provided in Sessions 3 and 4 for the K and I steps (e.g., fear of roller coasters):

So remember how I was saying I got nervous about roller coasters? And I worried that I might fall out of the cart? Well, do you know what kind of calm thoughts I had when I rode the roller coaster? I thought, "I've never actually heard of someone flying out of their cart . . . and the roller coasters have good seatbelts just like a car." In fact, I heard that it is as safe going on a roller coaster as it is driving in a car!

Ask the child if he or she thinks the therapist's calm thoughts helped the therapist feel calmer and less afraid in the situation. Provide feedback and discuss.

If the child volunteers a feared situation during or after this disclosure, help brainstorm on calm thoughts he or she could have used. Consider drawing or writing about the situations.

Review the first three steps of the KICK plan: *"Okay, let's try to remember what each step is. Okay, the K step was* [pause] *that's right, Knowing I'm Nervous . . ."*

Challenge task.

Assign the child Challenge 4. It corresponds to the K, I, and C steps of the KICK plan, and is intended to help the child contemplate the calm thoughts that might help the character in the cartoon.

With Parents and Child Together (10% of the Session)

Review the self-help skills assignment.

Briefly inspect the Self-Help Skills Diary (if the parents completed it) and inform the parents that their responses are very helpful. Ask for clarifications about how the self-help skills assignment actually went. Most commonly, children will have done the assigned tasks without difficulty. Occasionally challenges arise that must be addressed (e.g., by making the tasks easier).

Talk briefly with the child about what an accomplishment he or she made, assuming there was any success with the assignment. Emphasize the idea that the task was grown up or mature (according to the child's developmental level and personality) and ask if the child feels proud, noting that he or she should. Keep this lighthearted and note the child's reactions before overemphasizing the positive feedback.

Encourage the family to continue working on self-help skills, either (1) breaking down previously assigned tasks into smaller chunks so the child can experience partial success if something proved too difficult (e.g., have the child do all of the bathing routine by himself or herself except setting the water temperature and getting out of the bath); (2) increasing the child's level of independence in the skills already identified, or (3) adding additional skills for the child to work on.

With Parents; Child Optional (About 50% of Session)

Suggest that fear and anxiety can often lead to anger, disobedience, or aloofness.

Explain how fear and anxiety can lead to a variety of negative emotions and behaviors. Personalize this point for the family: (a) If the parents have provided relevant examples in previous sessions, refer to these specifically, and (b) if you have observed the child's coping responses in session, refer to these specific behaviors. Be sure to both describe the specific behavior and relate that behavior to its anxiety management function (i.e., how it represents a coping response because it reduces anxiety).

For instance, a child who is very scared of going to school may have angry outbursts in the morning because that behavior ultimately lets the child stay home from school. It is helpful to remind yourself that even though your child might be acting angry, this simply represents a coping response that your child has adopted to deal with anxiety. Your child is not being naughty—he is just very nervous and dealing with the situation the best way he knows how. We are teaching him new coping responses and the communication techniques that I am going to teach you today will help him develop these skills.

Teach the CALM approach to dealing with children's negative feelings.

Explain that when children are feeling anxious or upset, they have very little attention for dealing with conversation, logic, and suggestions. This is a result of how the brain deals with fear—when the emotion-center of the brain (i.e., the limbic system) gets triggered, everything else can be overlooked. Fortunately, because of the way the brain handles emotions, fear, anxiety, and anger go away slowly but surely. For example, fear shows a consistent decrease the longer a person stays in a feared situation, as long as they remain safe.

Point out that to help children learn to manage their fear and anxiety, it is important to be very calm and patient. Waiting patiently can provide children with an opportunity to learn that they are safe and give the KICK plan a try. By taking time, one can help children develop new coping responses. Children need to practice their new coping skills when they are anxious without having problems solved for them.

Pass out the CALM handout. Review the steps on the handout and discuss them. Special emphasis should be placed on labeling feelings.

Acknowledge that many parents question the appropriateness of accepting negative feelings and behaviors. Address this in the following manner:

Remaining calm and labeling feelings when children are upset has two benefits. It allows the child to experience bad feelings without adding to the bad feelings—trying to talk kids out of bad feelings often makes the feelings worse. It also provides the child with a model of calm behavior. You show that you can cope with your child's feelings, and your child may slowly learn from your example.

Personalize this technique by describing how it would be used in a situation relevant to the family:

When Suzy gets mad in the morning as you try to get her into the car, she is experiencing anxiety—she is afraid of being separated from you. During these times it is important to accept her bad mood (when she is yelling at you), label her feelings (e.g., "You are really scared right now"), and show her that you are going to be patient with her—model for her how to be calm. That will help her develop new coping responses because she is able to learn about her emotions. Your behavior will help calm her down, and eventually you both will be able to more easily negotiate the morning routine.

Describe selective attention as an additional helpful technique.

Explain that a logical extension of the CALM approach involves not responding to certain anxious behaviors. It is important to avoid giving too much attention when children are feeling scared. This could cause the fear to become even worse by reinforcing it.

Pass out and discuss the Selective Attention handout. Emphasize that this is a good technique to use in situations in which the child has agreed to face his or her fears but is now trying to avoid the feared situation. It is used after labeling children's feelings and demonstrating a calm, accepting attitude toward the child. Explain that if the child remains anxious after CALM responses, selective attention can be used to reduce (a) tantrums, complaining, and negative comments; and (b) repeated questions and other irrational dialogue. This will help the child return to a lower level of anxiety.

Try to personalize this technique to situations relevant to the family. Here are some examples of situations well suited to selective attention:

- A child sits in the car outside of school and cries, begging not to go to class. The parent sits quietly and ignores the child's tantrum, waiting until the child has calmed down, and then reiterates the child's reward for going to school that day.
- A child won't get in line at McDonald's to order herself a hamburger due to social anxiety, and asks to go home repeatedly. The parent labels the child's feelings, explains that he expects the child to calm down before making any decisions, and then waits quietly.
- A child repeatedly states that his homework is too hard, he can't do it, he hates it, and he needs help on every problem. The parent feels frustrated, acknowledges the child's anxiety, and then excuses herself, explaining that she would like the child to try the next 20 problems and she needs to take a break and will check on him in a while.

Warn the parents that these communication techniques may not feel natural at first.

Most parents feel awkward and unnatural the first times they try labeling feelings, waiting patiently or ignoring, and not responding with advice, suggestions, and so forth. This is to be expected. Most find that they have to try this approach with their children several times before it begins to feel smoother and more genuine.

Assess the parents' reactions.

Ask the parents how the child might respond to these techniques. If they express doubt or disagreement, try to identify and respond to their objections. Refer to the Common Parental Reactions section below for guidance.

Ask the parents how they typically feel when the child becomes anxious or worried. What do these feelings make them feel like doing at these times?

Problem solve with the parents about where they think they might run into difficulties with these techniques. What kinds of situations would make it hard to use these techniques? How has the child responded in the past? Do the parents' own feelings in some situations with their child make it difficult to follow the CALM steps?

Common Parental Reactions and Therapist Responses

I think it's important to help the child see that these worries are not rational.

The problem can be talked through rationally later, after your child is calm again. However, children are not able to understand things rationally or learn well when they are upset. There is a time for everything—many parents find that it is helpful to talk with their child and problem solve after the child is calm again. While the child is very upset, the best response is simply accepting and labeling the child's emotions and listening to the child. Remember the phrase, "If you resist, feelings will persist; if you accept them, they will desist."

For instance, if a child is angry about having to go play with another child in his class, and is yelling at his mom that it's not fair, this is not the time to explain that you want to help the child develop more friends. That can be done later. For now, a simple "Gee, you're really upset," or "I can tell you're really worried about playing with Tommy" is what will most help the child.

My child needs to know it is not acceptable to behave in such a negative way. I can't condone that behavior by acknowledging and accepting.

Many parents feel uncomfortable with letting their child express negative feelings toward them, such as sarcasm or anger, especially when they yell or whine. Parents often want to express disapproval or explain why it does not make sense for the child to be upset. However, when kids are fearful or angry, they are not able to take in this kind of information. What they need is a chance to let out the negatives without someone trying to resist or change their feelings.

Of course, all parents have to decide on their own comfort level. Some parents find that they can come to tolerate children yelling and complaining as long as the child is not rude to the parent or other family members. When your child is having negative feelings and says something like, "You're mean," many parents have had success by clearly and calmly stating, "I don't like that. I can tell you are feeling nervous, but you still need to be respectful." Other parents feel comfortable just labeling the child's feeling: "You are really mad right now."

By accepting the child's worries, are we promoting them and making them persist?

It is important to emphasize that we are only accepting the child's feelings, not the behavior. You are not saying, "It's okay to avoid school" or "I accept you yelling at me." You are saying that you accept the child's bad feeling and can handle it. Feelings are always okay, but negative behaviors are not.

I label his feelings already, but he doesn't stop feeling anxious!

Negative feelings don't go away automatically or respond every time you demonstrate your acceptance. Many parents find that they have to wait awhile. Patience is required and is a key to the CALM strategy. Children do not completely overcome their anxiety with the use of this technique—it simply reduces some of the anxiety. It is part of the overall strategy that we use to help children with their anxiety, and in combination with the other parts of the treatment, it is very important. For instance, being patient and waiting allows children to begin practicing their calm thoughts—something children did not know how to do before starting the program. The different treatment strategies work together to reduce the child's anxiety.

Ignoring my child when she is crying, yelling, or repeating herself is impossible!

Many parents feel self-conscious if children become upset in a public setting. It can often feel embarrassing and makes many parents want to avoid situations where it might happen again. It is important to know how you tend to react in these situations in terms of your own feelings, so that we can think constructively about how to make these situations more tolerable.

HANDOUT

Challenge 4: Give Me a Hand!

FIGURE 4.18.

What did you notice about this boy's face that tells you how he is *feeling*?

_____

This boy has a lot of icky (or irritating) thoughts. List two of them. Say what the thoughts might be. For example, don't just say, "Ninjas," but say something like, "He is afraid a ninja might get him." Think of two other icky or irritating thoughts that he has.

1. _____
   _____
2. _____
   _____

Give this boy a hand. What kind of calm thoughts would make him feel better? Think of a calm thought to help with each of the two other icky or irritating thoughts you just wrote about.

1. _____
   _____

2. _____
   _____

HANDOUT

Calm Strategy

Helping Children Cope With Their Feelings

Catch Your Breath (Pause to think or withdraw briefly to become calm and plan a response.)

Accept Negative Feelings (Wait patiently and respond to angry or worried comments with "Hmm . . . oh . . . I see.")

Label Emotions ("You seem really nervous.")

Model Coping Skills (Show your child, through your behavior, how to remain calm and collected.)

Example:

C: "I need a minute to think about this. Hold on a second, and then we can talk."

A: Wait patiently as the child complains about the situation. Express acceptance by nodding and using active listening: "Oh . . . I see . . ."

L: "Gee, you seem upset right now. Your face is red and you look really unhappy."

M: "This is a time when we could really use the KICK plan!" Engage the child in a discussion about applying the KICK plan to the situation. Or don't say anything. Just remain calm and keep in mind how helpful it can be to your child to have a chance to cool down and work through the anxiety on his or her own.

HANDOUT

Selective Attention

Avoid giving too much attention when children are upset.
It is very important to provide acceptance and understanding.
But too much attention can cause fear and anger to increase
and be expressed in the same circumstances in the future. To
prevent this, label the child's feelings in an accepting tone of
voice ("You seem scared . . ."). Then, use *selective attention:*

1. If the child expresses fear or anger, do not respond repeatedly. *Wait patiently.* Occasionally label the child's feelings in a calm voice without giving advice or suggestions. (Child: "You're mean!" Parent: "You sound angry.")
2. If the child asks repeated questions (such as, "You're coming home at nine o'clock, right?"), answer the question *once* and then remind the child that he or she already knows the answer—*or do not respond at all.*
3. If the child demands to leave a feared situation, *give a choice.* Remind the child that he or she needs to stay in or near the situation but has several options (such as, "You can either go into school, or wait here in the car with me for a bit longer").

Don't engage in lengthy conversations when children are really upset. When anxious, children cannot be convinced that things will be okay. Also, children usually ignore advice and suggestions when they are scared. Save logic and advice for a time when the child is calm.

SESSION 6

Develop the Exposure Hierarchy

BACKGROUND

Children with excessive anxiety avoid facing feared situations and do not learn that they can handle the situations without difficulty. The principle of exposure therapy is to gradually expose a child to increasingly difficult situations to counteract this avoidance and teach through experience that these situations are safe. As noted in Chapters 2 and 3, learning processes play an important role in the development of fears and in exposure therapy. Working through a hierarchy of feared situations helps reduce anxiety via slow habituation and allows children to practice new coping skills in modestly challenging situations without feeling overwhelmed. Exposures are instrumental for treating most child anxiety problems. The goal of this session is to set up an initial exposure hierarchy with the child and parents. Setting up a hierarchy with the family will take most of the session, so there is little time to discuss new problems in this session. Note that no exposures are assigned for homework until Session 7 because they need to be linked with the broader-based reward system developed in that session.

GOALS
1. Review the child's Challenge homework and rewards.
2. Teach principles of exposure to the parents.
3. Develop a hierarchy of the child's fears and anxieties.

PREPARATION AND MATERIALS

Photocopy Exposure Therapy and Feelings Thermometer handouts.

See the Appendix for multiple exposure tasks that have previously been used successfully with children in the Building Confidence program.

Review the diagnostic assessment materials from Session 1 for ideas about possible feared situations for the hierarchy. Make a preliminary list of 5 to 15 feared situations that range in intensity—these should reflect all of the major anxiety symptoms (including social phobia, separation anxiety, generalized anxiety, panic, and phobia symptoms) experienced by the child. For each of these 5 to 15 feared situations, create two or three steps that range in difficulty level. For example, for the general situation of fear of using the phone, three steps of varying difficulty might be: (1) calling a trusted person like the child's grandmother; (2) calling an old friend; and (3) at the highest difficulty level, calling a new friend to come over to play. These will be rated on the Feelings Thermometer by the family in the session and serve as a guide for the rest of therapy. The thermometer is an important CBT tool because it helps the therapist and family determine what is easiest and hardest for the child (and thus, where to start and end for each area of exposure) and offers a simple clinical tool for measuring improvement in anxiety during exposure therapy (see Session 8).

See Figure 4.19 for a sample hierarchy with fear ratings given by a family, and notice how there are several steps of varying difficulty for each general situation. It is very important that the hierarchy list include specific situations and not general descriptions (e.g., it is preferable to write "Touching my mom's socks and waiting 20 minutes to wash my hands," rather than, "Getting germs on my hands," which does not specify a particular behavior).

In preparing the preliminary hierarchy list, keep the following exposure methods in mind:

- **Exposures for feared or avoided activities** (e.g., dogs, playdates, talking to new people, attending school) generally

involve going into the feared or avoided situation, and exposure tasks are directly worded in this way: "Spending 10 to
15 minutes playing with other kids from class at recess,"
"Going to school for 2 hours each day, with Mom waiting in
the parking lot." When developing the hierarchy with the
family, the question to ask is: "How nervous would it make
you to . . . [e.g., be 5 minutes late to first period at school?]"
(see appendix for exposure ideas).

- **Exposures for perfectionism** (e.g., needing to be on time,
needing to get all A's, never be tardy) use the paradoxical
intervention of having the child intentionally fall short of
perfection; for instance, being late, not turning in assignments, not getting help on homework, or doing a poor job
on homework or test items. There is no need to justify to
the family the rationale for including such items on the list
at this time, although parents will need careful explanation
of the need for such exposures when they are conducted
later in treatment (see appendix for additional exposure
ideas for perfectionism).
- **Exposures for worries** (e.g., wondering if assignments will
receive good grades; ruminating over events of the day; worrying about keeping things tidy, clean, or in order; concerns
about homelessness) can also include paradoxical tasks
such as turning in poorly done assignments; intentionally
making a bedroom messy; or intentionally breaking a minor
rule (e.g., not talking in the library). Worries that cannot be
addressed with such an approach (e.g., worries about homelessness) can be addressed by focusing on positive thoughts
(a variant of the C step), as well as by engaging in behaviors
other than exposure (e.g., volunteering in a soup kitchen
with a family member) that allows the child to take action in
dealing with the worry. Sometimes exposures using the
child's imagination are appropriate for worries too (e.g.,
making up a story for the therapist that illustrates a worry)

and can be included on a fear hierarchy (e.g., "Telling Dr. W. a story about coming in second in the track meet"). Use of these imaginal exposures often requires the therapist and child to close their eyes together and take turns describing enough details of the story or scenario for the child to develop a mental image of the situation. After the child has become familiar with the worrisome image and thought, they are encouraged to change the visual image in a positive direction. An example relating to worries about homelessness might be that the child changes a disturbing image of a homeless person in degrading circumstances to the person receiving food at a soup kitchen in clothes from a thrift store, and later working behind the counter in a new job. Work with changing imagery of this kind can be very helpful in counteracting worries about situations that are out of a person's control (see the appendix for exposure ideas for worries).

- **Exposures for obsessions and compulsions** should be included but may need a special presentation. Often the task is for the child to not engage in a compulsion and to intentionally think about an upsetting obsession. For example, hierarchy items for a repetitive-question compulsion might begin with the child asking a question about the same topic no more than five times per day; then, in subsequent weeks, no more than three times; and eventually, no more than one time. Another series of exposures for compulsions might have the child spending less and less time per day organizing and cleaning an already tidy bedroom. If there are upsetting obsessions, children may need to think about them intently without engaging in compulsions or other safety behaviors (e.g., think for 4 minutes about a disturbing image without praying; draw a picture of the image; tell a story about the image). Often, an imagery-based imaginal exposure approach similar to that described above for worries is appropriate, in which the obsessive image is described and imagined, and then slowly altered to something less frightening or even humorous (e.g., a bloody axe becoming a large candy cane). Children often need behavioral tasks to confront obsessions (e.g., for obsessions about germs, children may need to use the bathroom without washing hands; touch various surfaces such as tabletops and doorknobs without cleaning their hands; see the appendix for additional OCD exposure ideas).

Carefully review the Exposure Therapy handout in addition to the instructions below. This form includes the key tips and important points to address with parents as well as ways of describing learning and reinforcement concepts to parents without using jargon.

SESSION

☞ **Therapist Note:** Prepare the child for the format of the session. After the meeting with the parent for a few minutes, the entire family will meet with the therapist for the rest of the session to make some plans together.

With Parents Alone (20% of the Session)

Introduce the purpose of the module.

When people face their fears, they often learn that they can deal with situations better than they expected, and they begin to feel more confident—they stop avoiding these situations. This is the single best way of reducing anxiety.

Pass out and review the Exposure Therapy sheet. Cover each point. Children increase their anxiety when they avoid situations that are actually safe (e.g., school, playdates, speaking with unknown people, staying with a babysitter).

Use examples of common situations like learning to swim to illustrate the method of exposure therapy. The concept of baby steps cited in the worksheet is important for parents to understand.

Note that the child is learning a plan for how to cope with anxiety—the KICK plan. Using a hierarchy of feared situations, ordered from easiest to hardest, the child will practice the KICK plan during the treatment sessions and at home. Explain to the parent that the child will begin with very mild situations and that this builds up confidence for facing harder situations.

Introduce the rationale for making a fear hierarchy.

Explain that the session will largely consist of setting up the fear hierarchy, which will act as the guide for future sessions. Therefore, it is important for most of the child's fears to be identified on the fear hierarchy.

However, it is preferable that the child not know that he or she will be facing the situations on the hierarchy for now. If the child knows, his or her anxiety ratings could be inaccurate. Inform the parents that you will keep the purpose of the hierarchy ambiguous while you are forming the list together.

With Parents and Child Together (80% of the Session)

Review the Challenge task.

Review the child's Challenge task. If he or she did not write responses on the worksheet, allow the child to complete it with you. Give gentle corrective feedback to clarify any misinterpretations. Record appropriate points or stickers on the reward chart.

If the child has earned four points or stickers, he or she should now receive the agreed-upon reward. Discuss with the family the importance of following through on the reward soon, and praise the child's hard work in completing the four Challenge tasks. Note that he or she will have opportunities to earn more rewards beginning next session.

Inquire about the self-help skills homework.

Ask about how the self-help skills assignment went. As in Session 5, talk with the child briefly about the importance of his or her accomplishment with any skills that were worked on. Encourage the family to continue working on self-help skills by either (1) breaking down previously assigned tasks into smaller chunks so the child can experience partial success if a task proved too difficult, (2) increasing the child's level of independence in the skills already identified, or (3) adding additional skills for the child to work on.

Set up hierarchy (this will take 20 to 40 minutes).

Explain that the parents, child, and therapist will need to work together to make an important list. Both parent and child will have a say in rating each situation.

Present and explain the Feelings Thermometer—it is used to rate situations in terms of how anxious or nervous they make someone. Describe it by providing samples of the two anchor points.

> For example, a "zero" might be something like eating a hot dog, watching TV, or taking a bath—no problem at all. You feel calm and not nervous. For me, a "10" might be like sky-diving—it would make me so nervous that I really wouldn't want to do it. What are some other examples of scary things most people would rate as a 10? . . . Right! So, what about these middle numbers, like five? What do they mean?

Explain that you will make a list of different situations, some of which will only cause a little anxiety, and some of which will cause a lot of anxiety. Using the list of feared situa-

161

tions you compiled before the session, explain that you have thought of some situations already and that the family may have additional suggestions or examples. Key pointers:

- Situations should be very specific (e.g., "Getting into bed without help and staying in own bed during night") rather than general ("Going to sleep in my bed").
- Most situations should be things that the child can do frequently (e.g., "Walking to school by myself") not occasionally (e.g., "Going to a friend's birthday party by myself").
- See the Appendix and Preparation and Materials for additional suggestions on what to target and how to word exposures of different kinds.

Using the preliminary list of feared situations that was prepared for this session, have the child make a rating on the Feelings Thermometer for each situation. Look to the parents for confirmation and allow them to interject if they have different feelings about the ratings of some situations. Encourage them to try to agree but let the child be the final judge for now, and do not waste too much time on the negotiation process. Write each ranking on the list of feared situations (you may want to retype these ratings onto the list later if you saved the preliminary list on the computer).

Congratulate the family on a job well done and let them know you will be talking more about the KICK plan as well as more rewards next session.

	Fear Rating
Separation anxiety: spending time alone	
Spending 10 minutes alone in my room.	3
Watching a movie or engaging in an activity for 1 to 2 hours without checking where mom/dad/sister are.	6
Going to public bathroom alone.	10
Separation anxiety: spending nights in own bed	
Spending no more than 15 minutes in bed with parents.	5
Only spending 5 minutes in bed with parents.	7
Sleeping in my own bed all night long.	10
Social phobia: getting to know new kids	
Smiling and waving to at least two classmates per day.	2
Asking if I can join a game on playground and playing for at least a few minutes.	6
Playing with kids through an entire recess.	8
Social phobia: making friends	
Saying hi to a possible friend at least once per day.	3
Getting the friend's phone number and calling her to ask about homework.	8
Inviting this friend over for playdate.	10
Generalized anxiety: worries about school	
Not complaining about going to school (one exception allowed).	5
Not asking questions about when school will begin.	7
OCD: violent images (eagles and bats biting her)	
Looking at pictures of eagles or bats for 5 minutes (no praying).	4
Writing a story about eagles or bats biting people (no praying).	7
Listening to tape of story about bats biting people (no praying).	9
Imagining bats biting people without trying to distract myself.	10

FIGURE 4.19. Sample hierarchy.

HANDOUT

Exposure Therapy

Children's fears are unrealistic: Children tend to fear situations that are actually safe. Examples:

- Many children fear being away from their parents even when they are in safe places such as school or at a friend's house.
- Others fear saying the wrong thing, so they avoid speaking in public or talking to new people.
- Some children have a lot of worries about day-to-day matters such as their homework or quizzes at school (even if they are doing well in school), about always being perfect and on time, their appearance, and so on.

Children need to face feared situations. It is never enough just to talk about how a situation is safe. Children can use logic to understand something is safe, but they will still experience anxiety until they see for themselves that they can handle the situation.

- As one example, children who avoid talking in public benefit from learning through direct experience that they are not humiliated by others when they give speeches. This experience allows children's beliefs about the danger of the situation to change: It is direct evidence—more than just an adult's opinion.

"Don't jump in the deep end of the pool first!" Although facing fears is the most effective strategy for fighting fears, it has to be done carefully. You would never try jumping in the deep end of the pool before learning if you can handle the shallow end, after all. Here are several key principles about exposure therapy (facing fears):

- **Take baby steps.** Ideally, every feared situation is broken down into a series of steps that the child can take to build up to the final target behavior. For example, a child who is very fearful of making phone calls might start by (1) calling a trusted person like his or her grandmother, then (2) calling an unknown person like a store clerk, then (3) calling an old friend, and (4) at the highest difficulty level, calling a new friend to ask him or her to come over to play.
- **Once is not enough.** In most cases, a single experience of any exposure to a feared situation is not enough to completely change a person's fearful beliefs. People might say to themselves, "Oh, I got lucky, but better not try my luck again." That is why multiple exposures to the same fear over the course of days and weeks are critical.
- **Use the KICK plan—this is what it is for.** To feel more confident about facing feared situations one baby step at a time, children should prepare and use a KICK plan each time before trying a feared activity.
- **Avoidance is not an option.** Avoiding feared situations strengthens the belief that the situation is dangerous and increases the difficulty children will face in "jumping back in the pool." When children attempt to face fears, they should not change their minds and back out at the last minute—this can make matters even worse.

HANDOUT

Feelings Thermometer

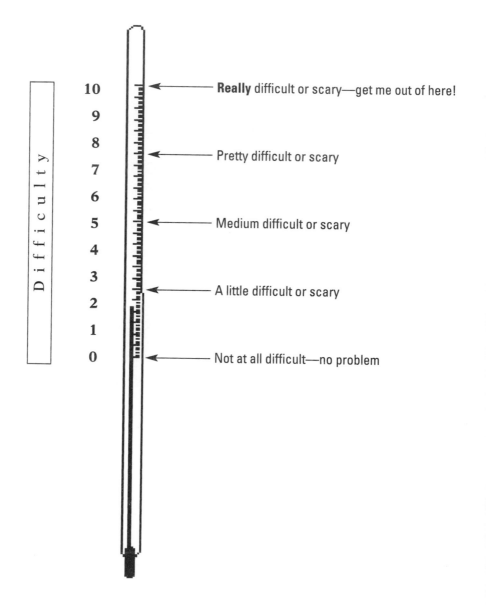

SESSION 7

KICK Plan: Second K Step, **Keep** *Practicing/Rewards*

BACKGROUND

Session 7 completes the presentation of the KICK plan. The concept conveyed by the second K step—Keep Practicing—is closely allied with the rationale of exposure therapy, which begins this session in the form of an easy Challenge homework assignment. Exposures can be thought of as a type of practice, such as practice trying out new situations and practice using the KICK plan. Many children like to think of the Keep Practicing step as synonymous with the phrase "just do it."

For the child, the transition to exposures can be slightly jarring. If not handled with care, the child could feel betrayed by the therapist. Children might think they have been tricked if they are suddenly asked to attempt difficult feared behaviors rather than continue to learn easily digested coping skills. However, a negative reaction to exposures can be avoided through a combination of steps.

First, the child's understanding of the concept of practice needs to be developed in this session. Examples must be provided that the child can relate to. Learning to swim is a particularly effective example for children who can swim. The idea is that one cannot begin swimming by jumping into the deep end; this would be dangerous and silly. One starts by putting a few toes in the water, testing it out, learning some basics about holding breath and kicking, trying out the shallow end with help, and so on. Once enough practice with the basics has occurred, harder aspects of swimming can be learned and mastered, and that is how one gets into the deep end and feels confident. This same logic can be applied to many other skills children can relate to if swimming is not for them, such as biking, reading, or playing the piano. Something that seems very scary at first—like the deep end—can become easy with slow practice and baby steps.

Second, a very mild initial homework exposure assignment should be given to the child—a task rated as a 0 or 1 on the 0–10 scale—to exemplify the Keep Practicing step at a level equivalent to putting toes in the water. Ideally, the child will have an amused and fearless reaction to such an assignment and respond with confidence. The child should, of course, help in selecting the specific assignment.

Third, to increase the fun of the exposure tasks and make it clear that there is a tangible and worthwhile payoff to the child for facing fears, a comprehensive reward system is set up. As noted earlier, reward systems are a critical aspect of effective CBT for children and are necessary the vast majority of the time for maximal progress to be made. Reward systems do not need to be maintained after anxieties are completely remitted through exposure therapy, although many families learn how useful they can be in addressing concurrent psychopathology (e.g., disruptive behavior) and choose to continue them even after the CBT program is completed. Caregivers should be encouraged to see rewards as well-earned compensation for hard work on the child's part, as facing fears is not easy. Since rewards are being used, the most motivating incentives from the child's perspective should be chosen. The effectiveness of any reward system is directly related to the consistency of its implementation and the perceived value of the incentives. Parents should be discouraged from restricting themselves to concepts such as natural consequences (i.e., rewarding a child who does not like to swim with a new bathing suit if he is willing to try swimming), because these approaches rarely employ highly motivating incentives from the child's perspective. However, the parents must be comfortable with the types of rewards that they are going to use. Leave some time to discuss potential pitfalls and help the parents develop comfort with the idea.

GOALS

1. Present the second K step of the KICK plan.
2. Teach principles of reward to the family.
3. Establish a list of highly motivating rewards.
4. Assign exposure Challenge homework to the child.

PREPARATION AND MATERIALS

- Carefully review the Just Rewards handout in addition to the therapist instructions below. This form includes the key tips and parameters for both aspects of this session, and includes important points to address with parents as well as ways of describing reinforcement to the parents without using jargon.
- Photocopy the following handouts: Challenge 5, Just Rewards, Rewards and Privileges Menu, My Challenges at Home.
- Bring the cartoons in Figures 4.3–4.15, including those that were used in Sessions 3 and 4.
- Bring the partially completed KICK plan sheet.
- Bring two pages of blank paper, pencils or pens of several colors, and crayons.

SESSION

With Parents Alone (30% of the Session)

Introduce the concept of rewards.

Pass out and review the Just Rewards sheet. Explain that doing exposure tasks (Challenge or practice tasks) is hard work. These tasks take a lot of concentration and energy. Just as with other kinds of work, it helps if people have something that they can work for. Use relevant examples: parents go to work to earn money and children do their schoolwork to get good grades so that they can get into college. Doing work in this program is similar, and we want to find things that children can work for that will give them motivation.

Review the pros and cons of using rewards versus privileges (or both) with the parents. It is often easiest if rewards include the simple point system described on the handout. For young children, consider a specific daily reward (e.g., an extra treat) for each time the child does an exposure. Parents should be cautioned not to use junk food as a privilege, however, out of concern for children's health and fitness.

Privileges may or may not need to have points assigned. If the child is earning the daily privilege of computers, TV, or some such by doing exposure tasks, then points are not needed. But if the child is working up to earn a special privilege such as a favorite meal, a trip to the park, or some other outing (something that would not be supplied on the same day), then points are needed and the privilege should be included on the child's reward menu.

Points should be arranged so that the child gets one per exposure. The points-per-reward formula should be calibrated so that the child can earn one or more small or medium items on the rewards menu each week if he or she does all of the assigned exposure tasks for the week. (Sometimes older children can delay gratification and work up to a larger reward over the course of weeks or months—but this is not recommended until a few small or medium rewards are earned first.)

Important: For now, do not make the child earn privileges that are currently taken for granted. However, if the child resists doing exposure tasks after a few sessions, do not forget that earning highly valued privileges that are currently taken for granted is an extremely effective means of encouraging compliance. Examples include daily TV and video game time, Gameboy time, computer time, use of art supplies at home, time outside skateboarding, playing with favored card games, or games related to the child's special interests.

Choose rewards that are highly motivating to the child, not the parents.

The child should help put together the rewards menu with the parents. However, the child may only earn rewards for which he or she has sufficient points—pleading and begging for a highly desired reward cannot substitute for points.

The parents should not negotiate with the child about rewards after the exposures. A specific number of points (generally one), or a specific reward or privilege, should be set in advance for each exposure. This is the only reward that should be provided for successful completion of the exposure—and it should not be taken away once it is earned.

Emphasize that when a child has done an exposure task, it is important to provide the reward on the spot if that was the agreement. Rewards are not given on the basis of whether the child did the exposure task perfectly but whether he or she tried hard.

With Child; Parents Optional (40% of the Session)

Review the KICK plan sheet briefly.

Ask the child to recall the first three steps.

Remember what K, I, and C stand for in the KICK plan? . . . Now we're going to learn what the second K stands for.

Introduce the second K step.

Introduce the fourth step, Keep Practicing. Write this step on the child's KICK plan sheet. Point out that the most important step to take after developing Calm Thoughts is to practice what to do in the scary situation.

171

What do we mean by practice?

If we haven't been in a swimming pool before, we start out practicing in the shallow end where our head can always be above water until we're sure we are good swimmers.

See Background for Session 7 and elaborate.

If we are going to give a speech in front of the whole class, we practice our speech a couple of times with our mom so we don't forget and get embarrassed when we're in front of the class.

Use other relevant examples that may resonate with the child's experiences and interests.

Initiate a conversation about the value of practicing by asking why it helps to practice when scared. Include the following points, trying to elicit each from the child through Socratic questioning:

- When we practice something difficult, we feel confident that we'll be able to do it.
- Practice is usually like taking little (baby) steps. Doing things a little at a time is always easier than doing a big thing all at once. The swimming example is excellent to illustrate this—not trying the deep end first.
- Practicing helps us know what to expect if we're going to be doing something new.

It is a good idea to practice with training wheels before riding a regular bike, for instance.

It is a good idea to practice an overnight sleepover with a friend before trying to go to an overnight summer camp for a week.

These are little steps that make the real thing easier.

Important: Note that many tasks that seem scary to some children (like going in the deep end of the pool) can seem very easy to them after they practice taking baby steps and building up to it. This is best if it is personalized to the child by focusing on a task that he or she has mastered that might be perceived as scary by younger children or novices.

> For instance, you're a great swimmer now. But do you think some kids who have never swum before would think the deep end is really scary? Yes, of course! But once they get good at holding their breath and learning their strokes, and then slowly try out the deep end—are they scared of it any more, or does it all of a sudden seem fun? . . . Exactly—things that seemed scary at first can turn out to be the most fun of all if we take small steps to get comfortable with them!

If there is time: Return to the cartoons used in earlier sessions. Briefly review the scenario of each cartoon with the child. Ask, in each case, how the cartoon character could practice or use little steps to get used to the scary situation (to learn that he or she can handle it and that it is safe).

If there is time: Return to the therapist's self-disclosed fear (e.g., roller coasters) from previous sessions. Brainstorm with the child how someone with that fear could practice taking little steps to overcome it (e.g., go on a merry-go-round; then a slow roller coaster, perhaps several times; then consider a faster roller coaster).

If the child brings up fears, initiate a discussion focused upon methods of practice. Do not, however, disagree if the child asserts there are no opportunities to practice in the case of these fears—move on rather than trying to prove this point for now.

If there is time: Develop a hypothetical scenario relevant to the child's fears that has not been discussed in detail thus far. Brainstorm with the child on creating a specific KICK plan—

each of the four steps—to help with the situation. A new cartoon may be useful as a visual aid.

> Let's pretend this boy here is afraid of closing his bedroom door at night. When his mom closes his door, he cries and begs her to keep it open. But he wishes he was brave enough to sleep with the door closed, like his big brother does. Let's make a KICK plan to help him! Let's see, the first K step is . . . what? . . . Yes, Knowing I'm Nervous. How do you think he might tell he's getting nervous? Maybe he gets a racing heart and breathes real fast when his mom closes his bedroom door? Okay, next step, I . . .

Briefly review the four steps of the KICK plan. Explain that the KICK plan can help you deal with things that make you nervous, and suggest that it is important to think of a KICK plan each time you feel anxious—before you start practicing with little steps.

With Parents and Child Together (30% of the Session)

Check in and review.

If there is time: Briefly check on the progress of the child's self-help skills.

Briefly review the concept of Keep Practicing if the parents were not present for the child's session.

Set up the first home-based exposure Challenge task.

Extending the idea of the second K step, explain that in this program, children will practice taking baby steps with some situations that were discussed in the previous session (the easiest ones to begin with), testing them out, and if things go well, moving on to take more baby steps.

> This will be more fun than you think because we're going to be talking about rewards in a minute!

Some children like the metaphor of a scientist:

This program involves testing if things are safe or not. Like a scientist, we start out with a guess or hypothesis—maybe we guess something will be a little scary but we can handle it. Then we test it out, like an experiment. Then we make our discovery—either it turned out to be not so great, or maybe our guess was right after all and it's just fine! Each week, we will do a few experiments—sometimes during the session, and sometimes at home for a Challenge task.

Engage the family in a brief discussion to choose the first one or two home-based exposures. Encourage the family to choose exposures rated 0–2 on the 0–10 scale. It is fine to suggest a few possible exposures that seem appropriately easy and perhaps lighthearted. Injecting light humor and a casual tone can be useful in this discussion.

The exposures should be easy for the child and have a high probability of success. The child should act confident and even cheerful about the exposures or else they are likely too hard.

Tasks that involve aspects of daily routines (e.g., answering the phone, going to school by oneself) should be practiced on several (e.g., 3) days; tasks that are more out of the ordinary (e.g., watching a scary movie) may be done only once or twice during the week.

Emphasize the importance of the KICK plan for preparing for these exposures. Encourage the child to develop a specific KICK plan for these exposures (see Challenge 5 handout).

Discuss in some detail what the child and the parents will do in the home-based exposures. Plan specific dates and times.

Remind the child that this is the Challenge task for the week and that he or she will earn points that build up to rewards each time he or she practices the task this week.

Introduce the reward system to the child.

If rewards are being used, explain that the child will have the opportunity to earn "stuff you like" for doing Challenge tasks in this program.

If only daily privileges (such as earning TV time) are being used, parents should be involved in explaining this new expectation to children, so parental ownership and authority over the policy are established, and to protect the therapeutic alliance.

Brainstorm rewards or longer term privileges, as needed (if the rewards system will involve more than just earning daily privileges such as TV time).

Have the family develop some initial ideas about rewards and privileges on the Rewards and Privileges Menu. Suggest that the family think more about this at home and report back to the therapist next session.

Help the family assign point values or arrange a reasonable ratio of rewards to exposures, based on the type of rewards and privileges that are included on the menu (e.g., trivial rewards such as a cookie versus big rewards such as going to a restaurant or ballgame). Keep in mind the general points formula noted above.

Suggest that the family set up a weekly points chart to keep track of assigned and completed exposure tasks, and corresponding points. This can be kept on the refrigerator or in any spot that the family finds suitable—but there should not be any opportunity for the child to be tempted to cheat and add points (parents might write their initials on the sheet for each point earned). Give the parents the sample points chart (My Challenges at Home) and encourage them to set one up on their computer and update it each week according to the assignments being given.

Discuss the rewards and privileges that could result from the current week's exposure tasks.

Help the child and parents understand how points, rewards, or privileges will work for the current week's assignment. Walk them through the logic so they understand what to expect and when the reward has been earned. Using an appropriate affective tone for the child, note that you are excited that he or she is going to get a chance to earn some "cool stuff," and that this is just the beginning—the child can earn even more points in a few weeks.

Give the child the Challenge 5 handout, filling in the top line describing the nature of the exposure tasks as well as the lines specifying the number of days and the nature of the reward.

Ask the family to bring the point chart and the Rewards and Privileges Menu each session to help you assess the child's progress and determine what steps to take next.

HANDOUT

Just Rewards

1. **Compensation for hard work:** Facing fears takes a lot of concentration and energy. Children are unlikely to think facing their fears is valuable or enjoyable (until they experience the results firsthand). Just as with other kinds of work, it helps if people have something that they can work for. Therefore, to keep children's motivation, enthusiasm, and participation at a high level, they need some kind of compensation. Compensation for hard work is not a bribe.
2. **Rewards and privileges** are an essential part of CBT—they are well-deserved from a child's point of view. Here are a few tips for making them work as a therapeutic tool.
   - **Rewards are used in the short term for the duration of therapy** to get children to face their fears. The great thing about fears is that once children find out that a situation is safe, the fear generally goes away permanently. Therefore, rewards are only needed to encourage the child to face the situation until he or she feels comfortable in it. Rewards do not need to be continued when a child's fears subside.
   - **Rewards and privileges are an extremely effective child behavior management tool**—more fun for everyone than yelling and arguing. The same approach that we use in this program can be used to encourage children to engage in any important educational or social task that they are reluctant to try.
   - **Choose rewards and privileges that are highly motivating to the child.** It goes without saying that a new pair of socks is unlikely to motivate children to face their fears.
   - **Follow through every time.** Whatever reward or privilege you select, try hard to come through on your end of

the bargain, on time. If a cookie was promised right after the child makes a phone call, for instance, it will not help matters to wait until a trip to the store the next week to get the cookie.

- **Never give the reward if it was not earned.** For example, if the reward is TV time after school, children should not be allowed to watch TV until they do their Challenges.
- **Rewards and privileges encourage children's independence.** Generally, if the reward system is working (with motivating rewards and privileges on the list), children can make up their own minds about whether to do their Challenges or not. They will usually feel motivated to do them, but this provides them with the sense of having had a choice.

3. **Distinction between rewards and privileges.**
   - **Rewards:** Small items that your child can earn for engaging in a specific behavior or set of behaviors. Generally, give 1 point or sticker for each exposure task that is completed. The rewards menu will have a specific price (in points) for each item, so your child can earn a reward one or more times per week for doing all of the Challenge tasks that we assign for the entire week.
   - **Privileges:** Can be even more effective than rewards. With this approach, children must do their daily Challenges in order to earn the privilege of doing favored activities such as watching TV or playing on the computer. Privileges can also involve going special places, staying up 20 minutes later than usual, having a favorite meal, engaging in a special activity (e.g., baking a cake)— as long as the child only gets the privilege by doing the Challenges each day. Activities like this can be incorporated into the point or sticker system mentioned above. Only include privileges you are comfortable with.

Rewards and Privileges Menu

DAILY REWARDS AND PRIVILEGES

1. _____

2. _____

3. _____

4. _____

SHORT-TERM REWARDS AND PRIVILEGES

1. _____

2. _____

3. _____

4. _____

LONG-TERM REWARDS AND PRIVILEGES

1. _____

2. _____

3. _____

4. _____

Challege 5: Start Practicing!

This week I am going to try this Challenge:

_____

I am going to try it on _____ different days!

If I try this Challenge, my reward will be _____ .

Even though it might be pretty easy, I am going to practice making a KICK plan for it. If I cannot think of a real icky or irritating thought, I can make one up by imagining what other kids might worry about if they tried this Challenge.

Here is the KICK plan I will use each time I try this Challenge:

K _____

I _____

C _____

K _____

My Challenges at Home

Task	WED	THU	FRI	SAT	SUN	MON	TUE
Call a friend to invite him over (2×/week)							
Starting homework by myself, with great attitude!							
Staying in my room by myself while Mom's in the kitchen for 20 minutes							

Each task = 1 point

This week, if I get _____ points, I'll get to choose a medium reward!

SESSIONS 8–15

Exposure Therapy

BACKGROUND

This session is repeated eight or more times in a typical course of CBT to help children work their way up the fear hierarchy. The therapist and the family brainstorm on which exposures to introduce at each session to make timely progress toward eradication of the child's most significant fears and anxieties.

Two types of exposure tasks are typically conducted during Sessions 8 through 15: in vivo, in-session, exposures during therapy sessions and homework Challenge exposures throughout the rest of the week (of course, some homework exposures actually take place in school or other settings). Although in vivo exposures during the session are quite helpful, the most important exposures are the ones assigned for the child's daily environment—at home, school, and other relevant settings. This is partly because it can be difficult to find an analogous task that can be done in the therapy office that resembles a situation that the child actually fears (e.g., going to school, sleeping alone). Furthermore, by practicing at home and in other settings on a daily basis, the anxiety reduction process is likely to be more rapid than if exposures are only conducted in the weekly therapy appointment. Therefore, carefully planning out the homework Challenges for the week represents a critical aim and an especially worthwhile use of therapy time throughout the exposure therapy process in Sessions 8 through 15. Conducting successful exposures is the key to reducing the child's anxiety.

In vivo exposure is conducted during therapist-child meetings in Sessions 8 through 15 when time permits. The advantage of in vivo exposure is that therapists ensure that exposures are completed; they have a chance to see how the child reacts to feared stimuli, which helps with treatment planning; and they can initiate particularly hard exposures that parents are unlikely to supervise successfully.

Optional Additions—Family Therapy and Playdate Modules

Three family therapy topics can be useful as clinical supplements during the exposure therapy process. These three topics are discussed in detail in the Optional Family Therapy Modules. Each topic can be covered in a 20–30-minute block during a session otherwise devoted to exposure therapy planning (i.e., the session content described below). These family therapy topics can be covered if there is derailment of the exposure therapy process or if family dynamics or communication patterns appear to be playing a particular role in the child's anxiety.

Another useful clinical supplement to consider for some children is the Playdate/Friendship Module. Because anxiety can have a negative effect on children's social adjustment, many children with anxiety disorders can be socially isolated. Loneliness can intensify feelings of anxiety, but this can often be remedied by a carefully planned campaign of playdates. Because the playdate module is fairly long and complex, it should be done in lieu of an exposure therapy session during Sessions 8 through 15. However, bear in mind that playdates with new peers are likely to be anxiety provoking for many children and therefore do represent a type of exposure, requiring the same sort of planning and care that is given to other exposures.

GOALS
1. Review Challenge homework.
2. Prepare a KICK plan for an exposure—either in vivo or for a Challenge homework task.
3. If time permits, conduct an in vivo exposure.
4. Brainstorm on which homework exposures to work on next and how to conduct the exposures.

5. Optional—cover a family therapy topic (Optional Family Therapy Modules A, B, or C).
6. Assign Challenge exposure tasks for homework; link with rewards and privileges.

PREPARATION AND MATERIALS

Review the fear hierarchy in advance to develop ideas for what exposures might be covered this week. Be sure to consider ways to reduce the level of difficulty of an exposure without allowing the child to completely avoid it in case the child finds the initial exposure ideas too difficult. Bring the child's hierarchy of fears to the session as well.

Examples of in vivo exposures that can be done that take advantage of opportunities in a typical office setting include asking the secretary a question; looking silly (e.g., with ruffled hair) and walking through the building; tripping and stumbling on purpose in front of people in the waiting room; staying in a room by oneself (perhaps with lights off) or going somewhere safe out of eyeshot of the therapist; making phone calls; or disappointing someone (e.g., borrowing a pencil from a confederate and bringing it back broken).

Remember that in vivo exposures can involve imaginal exposures that take place in the therapy room (i.e., exposure tasks that involve imagining feared situations), if that approach appropriately addresses the child's clinical needs (see Session 6 for additional background on this topic). Methods of imaginal exposure for children include drawing a feared situation, writing or recording a story about a feared situation, listening to a tape recording of a story about a feared situation over and over, or closing one's eyes and imagining the visual, auditory, and other sensorial aspects of a feared situation and describing them out loud. Imaginal exposure is useful in the following situations: (a) building up to confronting a real situation, or (b) habituating to an upsetting memory (e.g., of abuse or trauma) or an obsessive thought (e.g., a thought that the child routinely struggles to avoid). It is especially important to use calm thoughts before and after imaginal exposures to help the child distinguish between imagination and reality (e.g., "That will never happen to me again. I am safe with foster parents now. I can handle remembering it") or think differently about the topic (e.g., "Just because I have thoughts about the devil doesn't mean I'm going to hell—a lot of good people like Jesus have thought about and talked about the devil. It doesn't mean I'm bad"). Furthermore, changing the imaginal story to a benign plot during the exposure process is very therapeutic, particularly when the mental imagery is explicitly altered (see Session 6). Sometimes this can be especially effective when it is humorous. One boy had an obsessive thought about throwing a baseball so hard at his father that it killed him (despite having an excellent relationship with his father). After various imaginal exposures focused on helping the boy habituate to this thought, he was encouraged to change the image so it became a large marshmallow that he was throwing at his father. He would imagine this, laugh, and say it was hard to take it seriously anymore. (See Appendix for additional exposure ideas.)

Bring the following handouts: Challenge _____, Feelings Thermometer, KICK plan written by hand.

Bring blank paper and pen to write down new exposure assignments and updates of the rewards system.

SESSION

With Child; Parents Optional (50% of the Session)

Review the exposure rationale (if not previously done).

Point out that many of the situations we are afraid of are actually safe (review salient examples). The way we "teach our brain" not to be afraid anymore is to practice being in the situation until we stop feeling afraid. Cite relevant examples previously discussed, such as learning to swim. Connect this idea with the Keep Practicing step of the KICK plan.

For older or bright children: Demonstrate in graph form that when we enter a situation that makes us fearful, our feelings of fear initially increase, making us want to leave; but if we stay and teach ourselves that nothing bad will happen, the feelings of fear start to decrease—somewhat gradually—until we feel not too fearful.

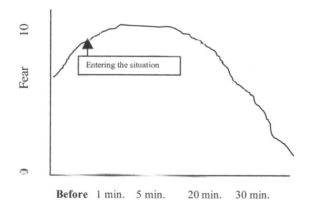

Decide on a specific in vivo exposure with the child.

As noted above, it is important to have several ideas prepared in advance for possible in vivo exposures. These exposures need to be feasible during the session; must be within several fear-rating points on the hierarchy of what the child has accomplished to date; can make positive progress toward advancing a general theme of in vivo exposures (e.g., reducing hand washing in small steps); or can broaden the child's experiences with exposures into areas the parents have not tried.

The child may give input on choosing between several reasonable in vivo exposures. However, refusing all proffered exposures is not acceptable. For many children, a friendly conversation clarifying the importance of exposures and how helpful it will be to the child to feel happy (e.g., confident, not afraid) in the specific situation are enough to elicit an agreeable attitude. For others, it may be necessary to note that the child is earning points for doing in vivo exposures (if this fits with the reward-privilege system in place), or arrange a short-term reward on the spot (e.g., time on the office computer, a treat). Finally, it is sometimes necessary to brainstorm with the child on how to reduce the intensity of an in vivo exposure to make it more acceptable.

Prepare for an in vivo exposure.

Develop a KICK plan for the exposure. Use the handwritten KICK plan sheet as needed to aid preparation. Use the review procedures described in Session 7 as needed.

Step 1. K Step—Focus on the physical cues of anxiety the child might experience in the situation.
Step 2. I Step—Review the irrational thoughts that the child harbors (or "some children would have") about the feared situation. Use Socratic questioning as necessary to help the child explain what he or she is afraid will happen.
Step 3. C Step—Identify calm thoughts to counter each of the irrational thoughts. Make sure that the child puts the coping thoughts in his or her own words.
Step 4. K Step—Review the concept of Keep Practicing. Scary things become easier when we practice. Some children like to say, "Keep practicing—just do it!"

Get a rating on the Feelings Thermometer before the exposure.
If needed (based on the child's need to practice and gain confidence or remember things to say in the case of any exposure involving a social interaction), take turns role-playing the

exposure situation (in the therapy room). The therapist can go first and pretend to be the child if this is helpful; then the child can try role-playing the situation.

Conduct the in vivo exposure and obtain a second rating from the child.

Go to the site of the exposure and either model doing the exposure so the child can see it done, or allow the child to give it a try immediately.

If the opportunity arises to ensure the situation is a success without the child knowing that the therapist intervened, it is generally a good idea to do so. For instance, it is permissible to wink or smile at a stranger or confederate to elicit the desired response. An exception would be times when the child is to be exposed to a situation that is intended to be unpredictable—in other words, a truly realistic exposure. Remove the child from the situation only if significant failure has occurred and there is little chance of turning it around in the short term.

When done, have the child make a rating on the Feelings Thermometer regarding (a) how fearful the situation actually was and (b) how fearful it would be to do the exposure again. Be sure to draw the child's attention to a drop in ratings of 2 or more points.

A drop in ratings should be the basis of a brief discussion reviewing whether the child's Icky Thoughts (fearful cognitions from the I step) were justified, or whether the Calm Thoughts (C step) were more realistic. This is a very important step in helping the child change the underlying anxious cognitions supporting the fearful response.

A minimal or negligible drop in fear ratings (unless the exposure was initially rated quite low) requires a careful review of the facts of the situation with the child: Did anything bad actually happen? If so, how bad was it? If not, how likely was it to possibly have happened? Brainstorm together on what steps need to be taken to make a future exposure easier, perhaps by reducing the level of difficulty (e.g., the number of steps involved, the length of time, or the specific location). Try to change the child's attitude from defeatist to optimistic by focusing on the ability to handle a modified version of the exposure.

If there is time, conduct another in vivo exposure.

Often an in vivo exposure should be repeated multiple times in the same session without any additional preparation. As an example, if the child had success in asking for the time from one individual, it is advisable to solicit his or her fear ratings and then repeat the same basic exposure several times. If the fear rating is going down, the exposure can be changed to a slightly harder version of the same exposure (e.g., asking for directions) with minimal additional preparation. Doing so maximizes the benefit of in-session preparation efforts and is often easier than trying to prepare for and conduct a completely different type of exposure in the same session.

Optional Alternative

Some therapists find it difficult to conduct in vivo exposures each time in Sessions 8 through 15 due to a shortage of time, the need to more thoroughly discuss home-based exposures with the family, or the need to include Optional Family Therapy Modules A–C in the session.

In sessions in which in vivo exposure is not possible, an alternative, briefer, meeting with the child can involve the following components and still address the same overall goals:

- Review the purpose of the home-based exposures (as at the beginning of the session).
- Develop KICK plans for the upcoming home-based exposures for the week, encouraging the child to take as much responsibility for thinking of the specifics for each step as

possible. Pay careful attention to the level of insight the child shows about icky thoughts and calm thoughts, and ask Socratic questions or model additional types of thoughts to help the child refine cognitive restructuring abilities.

- Role-play one or more of the planned home-based exposure situations. The therapist can model this first by talking through each step of the KICK plan in the role-play, taking the role of the child:

Let's see, K, Knowing I'm Nervous . . . well, all these butterflies in my stomach tell me that! Hmm, I, Identifying Icky Thoughts. Well, I guess a robber or kidnapper could come in my window while Mom's in the other room, and it makes me want to get out of this room right now! Okay, C, Calm My Thoughts. I've never actually heard of any robbers in my neighborhood—oh, and my parents are close by to protect me anyway. So the icky thought is pretty unlikely. K—Keep Practicing. "Just do it!" Okay, that means I'm going to stay in this room until the time is up—and that way I can earn my points for the day.

Then the child can take a turn role-playing the situation, with or without the narrative KICK plan dialogue.

- Address any other concerns the child has about the upcoming exposures in a friendly manner.

With Parents and Child (50% of the Session)

Optional—if Optional Family Therapy Modules A, B, or C are going to be covered in this session, begin the parent-child meeting with them, setting aside at least 15 to 20 minutes to cover one of these modules in sufficient detail.

Review exposure homework (weekly Challenge tasks).

Ask to see the points chart that the parents created (i.e., following the model given to them in Session 7) as well as the current Rewards and Privileges Menu. If they did not bring it, remind them to bring the chart and menu each time.

Ask the parents and child to report on the past week's homework Challenge exposures. If the system is working well, most of the assigned tasks should have been completed and most points earned.

For each assigned task from the previous week, have the child rate it on the Feelings Thermometer (p. 166) in terms of difficulty or anxiety if the child had to do the task again. Note the revised rating and compare it with the previous rating. A drop of at least a point or two indicates progress is being made and some habituation is probably occurring.

Any problems with completing the exposures should be carefully analyzed: Was the homework assignment too difficult or was there insufficient motivation? If the former, brainstorm an easier version of the exposures for the coming week (in the context of exposure planning, below). In both cases, the use of effective rewards and privileges should be discussed (see rewards program check-in, below).

Consider whether any exposures can be taken off the list of weekly assignments. Sometimes a child has become habituated to facing a previously feared situation or has stopped engaging in a nonproductive habit (e.g., asking repeated questions about an area of worry) that was being suppressed as a form of exposure in previous weeks. The family should update the homework exposure list and rewards chart by removing such target behaviors. For example, a child may now eat lunch with a group of peers every day and enjoy it rather than fear it; thus, he or she no longer needs external rewards or encouragement to do this.

Brainstorm with the child and parents about upcoming exposures.

Beginning with Session 8, it is reasonable to assign three or four different types of Challenge tasks per day for exposure homework. As an example, a typical set of early exposures and rewards (see Challenge _ handout, which is used to write the weekly assignment) for a child with some social anxiety and some separation anxiety would be: "10 minutes alone in my room with the door closed each day—1 point each time; 20 minutes in my own bed before getting in my parents' bed each night—1 point each time; call Ian on Thursday to ask him for the daily homework assignment from Ms. Wright—5 points, one time only."

Remember, the goal is to get to the top of the hierarchy for each area of exposure. Do not stop with a "middling" exposure that would ideally culminate in a more challenging one (e.g., sleeping only part of the night in the parents' bed rather than not at all; calling a friend but not asking them over; asking 10 repeated questions a day rather than 2). It often makes sense to increase the difficulty level of homework exposures but stick within the same general area of exposure until the child's fear of even the most difficult version of a particular area of exposure has been extinguished (as exemplified by a fear rating of 0 or 1 about a previously highly feared activity such as sleeping alone for the whole night).

Nonetheless, it is important to avoid getting stuck in any one area of exposures (e.g., increasing class participation, giving speeches) while neglecting other important areas. Here are some considerations in determining additional exposures:

- By Sessions 10 or 11, it is important to directly or indirectly ascertain the parent's highest immediate priorities—anxiety related or otherwise. Some parents have social or behavioral goals that are not related to anxiety per se, but may still be amenable to a hierarchical behavioral program (i.e., a step-by-step plan augmented by rewards or privileges). For example, a child with little interest in peer interaction still needs to engage in such interaction to learn social skills, and many parents rightly view this as a high priority. Whatever the priorities are, it is desirable to target these goals in the hierarchy.

- Review the fear hierarchy. Consider how the child's anxieties impact day-to-day functioning and try to identify the areas of anxiety that are creating the most interference. For example, fear of participating in class is probably more important to focus on than fear of heights. Early in the exposure process, attempt to broaden the areas of exposure being assigned for homework to cover at least the child's key areas of impairment (e.g., low class participation, social avoidance at recess, avoidance of playdates) so that any particular difficulties in a specific area can be identified before too much time in therapy has elapsed.

Discuss your ideas for the upcoming homework Challenge exposures with the family. Use a problem-solving, collegial style and be prepared to modify assignments to ensure that the child is a willing participant and that the parents view the tasks as acceptable and doable.

☞ **Therapist Note:** There can be exceptions to the general principle that the child should be actively engaged in setting the level of difficulty and agreeing to the assignments. Sometimes anxiety can overwhelm children's judgment and slow them to a glacial pace in exposure progress. At other times a child may need one large increase in task difficulty to make significant progress (e.g., confronting a phobic object directly) that cannot be broken down any further. In either case, it is perfectly acceptable to simply set a reward or privilege of significant value to children as the outcome of participation in a given task. Remind them that it is their choice to try the task or not and that the reward or privilege is waiting should they decide to do it. Of course, parental follow-through on this type of quid pro quo is particularly important.

Have the child rate the agreed-upon new homework exposure tasks on the Feelings Thermometer.

Write the planned homework exposures for the week on the Challenge __ sheet. Fill in the correct Challenge task number in the blank space. Note the number of times each exposure should be completed over the course of the week (e.g., one time or once per day).

Rewards program check-in.

Having rewards that the child wants is a key for motivating him or her to continue with the exposure tasks. As a result, monitoring the reward system in each session is important.

Ask what rewards the child has earned lately and what he or she is hoping to earn.

Help the child and parents project how many points will be necessary to earn the next item the child wants. It can be helpful to say:

> Well, if you earn 20 more points this week, you'll get it! Let's see, that would mean you'd do this Challenge task five times, this one three times, and this one just once! Do you think you're going to be able to do it?

As appropriate, casually review the child's and parents' view of whether additional reward or privilege options are desired and, if so, which should be added. As necessary, modify the rewards list to exclude items or privileges that are not motivating to the child. Also, for rewards or privileges that the child has access to all the time, the parent can either control the child's access to them or exclude them from the list.

Remember, the most compelling rewards are usually privileges that are renewable, wanted, and already used frequently by the child (e.g., TV, computer, specific games). These should be added to the rewards and privileges list if there are signs of poor motivation or mixed therapeutic alliance. The simplest formula is, "As soon as your Challenge tasks for the day are completed, you earn your normal privileges with . . ."

Children who sail through a steadily progressing set of exposures that become more difficult over several sessions can generally proceed well through CBT simply by earning a few desired items periodically.

However, in most cases of inconsistent or slower progress, the use of daily privileges (like access to TV, video games, and computers) as an incentive offers a generally effective solution that can speed progress and—as long as parents take responsibility for setting the terms of these privileges—does not normally undermine the child-therapist relationship.

Note the points, rewards, or privileges that the child can earn for each of the weekly Challenge tasks in the right-hand column of the Challenge __ handout.

As needed *if the child has engaged in noncompliant or avoidant behavior around exposures.*

Review communication strategies taught in earlier sessions, ask about whether they may be effective, and, if so, brainstorm on how to implement them. Focus on giving choices, respecting the child's struggle, the CALM strategy, and selective attention.

As needed *if the parents express reluctance about exposures or rewards.*

Acknowledge that the exposures and rewards system can take a lot of work to implement. Encourage the parents to continue with the exposures and rewards program. Assure the parents that the child will benefit as a result of their efforts.

I understand that it is hard work to set up the opportunity for exposures. I want to caution you about the importance of following up on these tasks each week. This process helps children become more confident and feel less anxious, which is why you are here. If you can keep up with the exposures, your child is much more likely to benefit from our work together.

Reassure the parents that when children habituate to their fears, rewarding them is no longer necessary. Children will continue to naturally act more independently and courageously.

As needed *if an exposure requires parental involvement that the child should not be aware of.*

Ask the child to leave the room for a brief time so you can check in with the parents about her role in the program.

Discuss any relevant details regarding the setup for the upcoming exposures that should not be discussed in front of the child (e.g., the parent may phone a peer's mother to double check that the peer would like to have a playdate with the child before suggesting that a phone call be made).

HANDOUT

Challenge __: Keep Practicing!

This week I am going to try these Challenges:	I'm going to do them this many times this week:	Points or rewards for each time:
_____	_____	_____
_____	_____	_____
_____	_____	_____
_____	_____	_____

Here is my KICK plan for one of these Challenges. I will remember to think of a good KICK plan before I do each one of my Challenges!

K _____

I _____

C _____

K _____

OPTIONAL FAMILY THERAPY MODULE A

Family Problem Solving

BACKGROUND

This module is intended to be implemented during the family meetings in Sessions 8 through 15 (see the Session 8–15 plans), generally taking a minimum of 20 minutes of a session. Like the other optional family therapy modules (i.e., Talk Time and Finding New Roles), this module can be used on an as-needed basis in cases in which progress in exposures is slow and family dynamics may be playing a role.

The philosophy of the Building Confidence intervention is that a high density of well-designed exposures is the key curative element for most child anxiety disorders. However, family interaction patterns (e.g., arguing, power struggles) and the emotions and motivations underlying such interactions may be curtailing the implementation of exposure activities. A number of interventions included within this program are designed to improve family communication patterns to potentiate successful exposures. This module focuses on family problem solving, which is designed to help improve parent-child communication about disputed topics. A key element of family problem solving is that each family member's opinion about a specific problem is given respect and accepted without judgment to reduce feelings of resentment and disenfranchisement in the child and parents. A core principle of problem solving is to think of all of the possible solutions to any problem before making any decisions about what to do. Family problem solving may be used to analyze where a family is getting stuck with exposure assignments and elicit solutions from each family member that might work for everyone, creating a sense of teamwork rather than animosity.

199

GOALS

1. Teach the family problem solving technique to the family.
2. Practice the family problem solving technique with the parents and child.

MATERIALS

Problem Solving handout

SESSION

With Parents and Child Together (25% of the Session)

Purpose of the module.

Remind the family that much of this program involves making plans together.

Today, we will learn how to use problem solving when we are making important plans together. We want to learn ways to compromise and find solutions that are acceptable to everyone in the family.

Describe situations when family problem solving can be useful.

Explain that the idea of problem solving is to figure out all of the possible solutions to a problem, and then choose the best one and try it out.

Suggest that some of the best times to use problem solving are: (a) when one person wants to do something one way and another person prefers to do it another way (a disagreement), (b) when family members have to make a decision together, or (c) when someone's feelings are hurt.

Ask the family to think of a time last week when one person wanted to do something one way and another person wanted to do it a different way. Probe for any disagreements or difficulties that were experienced during the child's exposure tasks during the past few weeks. Prompt them to think of very small or minor problems if they deny any recent disagreements. Ask the involved family members to describe what happened. Try to keep the conversational tone light or humorous, if possible. Emphasize that each family member perceived the situation in his or her own way.

Teach technique of family problem solving.

Note that in the situation described by the family, and many others, it is helpful to try to work together to solve the problem, rather than have a long argument or an unresolved disagreement. This is where the concept of problem solving comes in handy.

Distribute the Problem Solving handout to each family member and discuss. It can be helpful to embellish the points on the handout with the following information:

- The idea is for the parents and child to formulate a plan for solving the problem. Parents should emphasize that they really want to hear what the child thinks and feels about the situation, and that the parents plan on taking his or her ideas seriously and making a bargain with the child.
- The objective is not for anyone to win the disagreement. The goal is to find a middle ground. This makes everyone more likely to stick to their part of the bargain, and shows respect to all participants.
- It is fine if the child says "I don't know" when the parents ask how the child feels (Step 1) or what solutions he or she can think of (Step 3). Children should not be pressured to contribute if they do not want to and the parents should simply move on to the next step. It is respectful to give everyone a chance to say what is on their mind if they want to.
- Parents usually initiate the conversation, and it is perfectly acceptable for them to move it along and offer constructive

ideas if the child does not have any. The main thing to avoid is dominating the conversation if the child has something to say.

Suggest that this strategy works when everyone is calm and in a mood to talk. However, even when people are slightly upset, this can be helpful. Help the family think of some times when this might have been a good strategy to try (personalize the presentation by referring to the example they provided earlier in the session):

> So, going back to that disagreement that you had the other day about whether the Challenge task was to stay in Maso's bedroom with the lights on or off—do you think you both would have been in the mood to try going through these steps together and figuring out a solution if you tried this before everyone got mad? Or do you think you would have wanted to take a little time off before trying to problem solve?

Practice the technique.

If the family had difficulty with the homework exposure tasks this week, this is the best topic to discuss. Otherwise, use any exposure-related disagreement that has come up in the past. It is best to begin with the therapist playing the part of the parent and the parent playing the part of the child. Involve the child in later role-plays if he or she is willing. Initiate the role-plays casually:

> Let's say that we're having that same problem, you [*parent*] are [*child*] and you didn't stay in your room with the light off for 5 minutes, but you still want to stay up to watch the special TV show. I'm the parent, and I feel like you should actually do what the therapist assigned to you before getting your special privilege. So, looking at the first step of

this worksheet here, I think I might say something like, 'Well, [child], I understand that you'd really like to see this show, but I am concerned that you haven't done the assignment and this is not going to help you feel calmer and get better at the KICK plan.' See how I stated my feelings of being concerned? How do you think you might respond if you were [child]?

Continue in this way with each step.

Give feedback to the family on their performance of the techniques. Try to provide two positive pieces of feedback and one area that could be improved.

☛ **Therapist Note:** Be especially attuned to interruptions or parents asking the child a series of closed-ended questions, both of which are to be discouraged.

Warn the family that it takes a while to master problem solving.

Because it is an important skill, note that problem solving will continue to be practiced in this program.

Next week, we will use problem solving again to help plan for the upcoming week's exposures and rewards.

HANDOUT

Problem Solving

One of the best ways to solve disagreements is to have family members sit down and talk together like members of a team. Practice these steps and see how they work for you.

Step 1. Everyone shares their thoughts and feelings about the problem. Try not to interrupt each other. Avoid giving lectures. Kids might not have a lot to say at first.

Step 2. Brainstorm together to identify all the possible solutions to the problem. Anything goes—be sure not to criticize or reject any solution at this point. Everyone should get a chance to suggest solutions.

Step 3. Summarize all the possible solutions and make a plan. Everyone discusses the ideas that they liked and did not like. Think about which ideas to try out. Try to reach a compromise. It is important that everyone feels comfortable with the solution. Remember to make a specific plan.

Helpful Hints
- Sometimes a quick solution cannot be found, and you will both need extra time to think it over. This is very normal.
- If children don't want to talk, a written note can get things started.
- You might need to do more problem solving later on the same topic.

OPTIONAL FAMILY THERAPY MODULE B

Finding New Roles

BACKGROUND

This module is intended to be implemented during the family meetings in Sessions 8 through 15 (see the Session 8–15 plans), generally taking a minimum of 20 minutes of a session. Like the other optional family therapy modules (i.e., Family Problem Solving and Talk Time), this module can be used on an as-needed basis when progress in exposures is slow and family dynamics may be playing a role.

It is important to help children with anxiety disorders find new roles in their family and social network. Whether the child is in the role of the baby of the family, family lightning rod, parent's therapist, or little professor, these roles reinforce developmentally inappropriate behavior that tends to maintain anxiety disorders. The baby has probably attracted excessive help and assistance (cf. Session 4) that reduces his or her self-efficacy and sense of independence; the lightning rod generates so much negative attention around anxious behaviors that these behaviors are unintentionally reinforced; the parent's therapist may have been overburdened with the parent's concerns and has difficulty regulating anxiety in the face of constant modeling of anxious thinking, yet feels important and needed in the role of the parent's confidante; and the professor has been rewarded for precocity that is endearing to adults but anathema to peers, creating a barrier to friendship that feeds shyness and reticence. It is helpful for all family members to become aware of unhealthy roles that children may be playing and to take steps to change them to developmentally appropriate roles. When children are given new roles in the family that break the pattern of reinforcements that unintentionally promoted their anxiety, they often live up to these roles and can outgrow the less healthy roles that they currently assume.

GOALS

1. Discuss what kinds of roles the child currently plays in the family.
2. Help the family change daily routines and catch the child in different roles.

MATERIALS

Finding New Roles handout

SESSION

With Parents and Child Together (25% of Session)

Introduce the purpose of the module.

Point out that one topic for today is finding new roles for the child. Children often get stuck in roles that make it harder for them to overcome their anxiety. A great way of getting children out of roles is to help them have new experiences that contradict their old roles.

New roles (a) can help children see themselves in a new light, as more grown up, and as distinct from the old, more anxious selves; (b) can give children an increased sense of control of their life, which is helpful in reducing anxiety; and (c) can reduce family tensions and conflict. Be sure to personalize this presentation to the child's characteristics.

Describe the Finding New Roles handout.

Present the Finding New Roles handout to the family. Review the four types of roles with the family and help them identify which roles—if any—the child may have been playing.

Use your observations of parent-child interactions (e.g., child clinginess, the child as a source of the parent's anger) to guide your review of the child's role.

☞ **Therapist Note:** An important session goal is to identify excessive parent-child affection, which should be referred to as "your child's clinginess" (this terminology protects parents from feeling criticized for their own role in excessive affection). Observations of frequent physical affection may be gently referred to without generating parental defensiveness. This behavior is a manifestation of an immature or clingy role that parents can help change by changing their response to it. As in Session 4, this advances the structural family therapy goal of boundary reorganization in the service of eliminating problematic parent-child coalitions.

Personalize the presentation to the family by (a) focusing on areas of daily life that are relevant to the family, (b) emphasizing how having a more mature child might make life easier for the parents, and (c) acknowledging and accepting the parents' doubts and other negative feelings about changing roles.

Decide on several small changes in family interactions that could help the child develop more positive roles.

See the ideas for changes in communication patterns corresponding to each of the four roles on the Finding New Roles sheet and brainstorm with the family on additional changes that would be helpful in their daily interactions. Write these suggestions on the sheet.

Encourage the family to discuss the actual family interactions that will change this week to promote changing roles, as appropriate.

This topic can elicit anxiety in parents, who may be concerned that they have done something wrong. This may be expressed through the parents' questioning how the exercise is related to anxiety treatment. Emphasize that this program combines many different changes in the child's life, each of which helps the child cope with anxiety. No single exercise leads to an immediate cure, but when combined there is often notable improvement in the child's anxiety over the course of time. Finding new roles is an important step that builds toward a comprehensive shift in the way children handle emotions—partly because they expect a different set of behaviors and responses from themselves when they take on more age-appropriate, positive roles.

HANDOUT

Finding New Roles

Taking on new, positive roles can help children feel more mature and confident. It is helpful to catch children in moments that are inconsistent with their current role to guide them into healthier roles.

1. **Is your child seen as clingy, always needing help, or immature?**

   If so, are there times when your child does not play this role at home? Can you catch your child in confident, mature, calm, sociable moments and point them out with a proud smile? What else could you do to move your child out of this role?

   _____

   _____

2. **Is your child the center of negative attention or the family lightning rod?**

   If so, is it possible to keep your eye out for times that your child is acting the way you hope he or she would behave? During these times, let your child know that you're impressed with these positive behaviors and attitude. Say exactly what you like and make sure you don't undermine the compliment by saying that this is much better than usual. How else can you help your child out of this role?

   _____

   _____

3. **Does your child play the role of junior psychologist, often trying to solve family problems or listen to complaints about others' bad days?**

    This role is too mature for children and can be stressful. If this is the case, what can parents and siblings tell the child when he or she tries to play this role in the future?

    _____

    _____

4. **Is your child in the role of a little professor, often praised for being smart and precocious?**

    This role is rewarding to children, who love this sort of praise from grown-ups, but it can pose a barrier to peer friendship. Intellectual remarks that impress and amuse adults can seem arrogant and stuffy to peers. Family members can encourage a child to broaden topics and style of conversation to fit in the peer group. Ask what other children talk about, express genuine interest by learning about and talking about these topics with the child, and react with enthusiasm to topics of conversation or manners of speaking that sound age appropriate. Remember that it is possible to maintain intellectual excellence while still learning to fit in with the social world of one's peer group.

    _____

    _____

OPTIONAL FAMILY THERAPY MODULE C

Talk Time

BACKGROUND

This module is intended to be implemented during the family meetings in Sessions 8 through 15 (see the Session 8–15 plans), generally taking a minimum of 20 minutes of the session. Like the other optional family therapy modules (i.e., Family Problem Solving and Finding New Roles), this module can be used on an as-needed basis in cases in which progress in exposures is slow and family dynamics may be playing a role.

Children with high anxiety often fall into a negative role in the family in which much of the attention that they receive centers on their mood and behavior. For instance, a child with separation anxiety may become upset when other family members plan to go out, which can cause resentment in parents and siblings and trigger arguments. Some children engage in coping responses such as crying or tantrums that can negatively affect family members' reactions to them. At times, family members may talk about children with anxiety as being incapable of engaging in age-appropriate behavior. In each case, children fall into a pattern of receiving high levels of negative attention from their family. During the course of exposure therapy, relations can be even more strained when parents ask children to try various difficult tasks. Because of this emphasis on the child's problems, there is often a loss of positive interactions between the child and the parents. In light of the need to help the child find new, positive roles in the family (see Optional Family Therapy Module B), setting aside daily time for mutually rewarding parent-child interactions can be an important family intervention technique.

GOALS

1. Teach the parents Talk Time interaction skills.
2. Help the parents identify regular times for having Talk Time with the child.
3. Practice Talk Time with the parents and child.

PREPARATION AND MATERIALS

- Prepare a game or activity that the child will enjoy playing with the parents and therapist (a deck of cards is often sufficient).
- Make a photocopy of the Talk Time handout.

SESSION

With Parents Alone (10% of Session)

Briefly introduce the purpose of the module.

The focus of this module is finding ways to help the child develop a more positive role in the family that is unrelated to anxiety and other negative emotions.

Briefly describe the rationale of Talk Time.

Propose that one good way of addressing children's negative self-perceptions (e.g., "annoying," "a burden," "a worrywart,"— be sure to personalize this to the family) related to anxiety is to build up positive, mutually enjoyable activities and conversations that help children experience themselves in a positive light.

Suggest that it helps to start with daily parent-child time together in which the child sets the agenda and makes the choices. During this brief time each day, the child can experience positive feedback and feelings of control and enjoyment with the family.

Briefly teach the Talk Time techniques.

Review the Talk Time handout with the parents. Emphasize that the child should be given free reign to make choices about the activity and the rules of the game during Talk Time.

For two-parent families, emphasize that it is desirable for both parents to spend several days a week having Talk Time with the child.

Personalize for the family: (a) Inquire about which aspects of the technique seem best suited to the child, and (b) ask the parents if they foresee any major obstacles to engaging in Talk Time on a regular basis.

☞ **Therapist Note:** There is more than one way to have Talk Time. Point out that *all parents have unique ways to connect with their children.* Even if families do not foresee having frequent one-on-one time with the child (e.g., because the family is too large or busy), creative solutions can be found to meet the basic goal of Talk Time—positive one-on-one interactions with each parent. For instance, a parent could make an effort to sit down and chat with the child in a conversational way during breakfast each morning, or a same-sex parent could sit in the bathroom and chat with a younger child while he or she takes a bath at night. (The latter is often successful. However, as needed, politely point out that school-age children have privacy concerns—typically unspoken—regarding the opposite sex, including parents, which is why this suggestion applies only to the same-sex parent.)

Plan the use of Talk Time techniques.

Discuss with the parents what kinds of games or activities might be appropriate to try with the child for Talk Time (card games, building games like Lego, dolls or action figures for pretend play, or quick board games are often best). Get the parents' input on how to optimize the effectiveness of Talk Time for their child.

Tell the parents that these techniques can be used informally during a game that is planned when the child is invited back into the therapy room. Mention that there is no need to tell the child that the parents are practicing Talk Time skills; this will just be a good chance to try out the skills while they are fresh in the parents' minds. Note that the therapist will help model these skills.

With Parents and Child Together (20% of the Session)

Suggest that the therapist, parents, and child all play a game together.

Point out to the family that it is important to have fun together as often as possible, especially since the child is working hard on the Challenge tasks. Problem solve with the family to think of a fun game that everyone could play together for a few minutes. Encourage the family to try to spend time at home having fun together, too.

During the game, model Talk Time skills for the parents by speaking directly to the child with descriptive and reflective comments, and so on. Nod or provide other nonverbal feedback for the parents' appropriate use of Talk Time skills.

HANDOUT

Talk Time

TWO STEPS TO TALK TIME

1. Find 10 to 15 minutes when you are free and your child is playing alone or looking for something to do.
2. Join your child at his or her activity, or encourage your child to choose something fun for the two of you to do (avoid TV or computer games since they limit interaction). This should be one-on-one time—try to find a time when brothers or sisters are already busy.

DO's

Be a Sportscaster

Describe your child's behavior in a positive, energetic manner. Don't talk nonstop—just make periodic comments. For example: If your child is playing basketball, you could say, "He goes left, now he's dribbling low . . . a big spin . . . very tricky move there!"

Be a Mirror

If your child speaks to you about the activity, show that you are listening. In different words, repeat your child's idea or comment back:

Child: *Luke was a big bully at school today.*
Parent: *So, Luke was pretty mean today, huh?*
Child: *Did you see that shot, Daddy?*
Parent: *Wow, you sound so proud of that shot you just made!*

Let Your Child Take the Lead

Let your child choose the game, set the rules, and have a good shot at winning (if it is competitive). Try not to teach any new skills or lessons during Talk Time. Focus on giving positive attention and try to resist any temptations to coach your child or give advice.

DON'Ts

Don't Ask Questions

If possible, avoid asking questions. Even harmless questions can put kids on the defensive. Save up your questions for another time.

OPTIONAL SESSION

Playdate/Friendship

BACKGROUND

This optional session can be implemented anytime during Sessions 8 through 15 if the child is socially isolated and could benefit from more or better friends. Often the effects of this session emerge over the course of several weeks or more, as playdates take time to set up and exert positive effects, but this intervention can be quite powerful for children who have few friends or who are very shy. This session generally takes an entire therapy hour or longer to conduct, and it is difficult to combine it with a second Building Confidence session in the same meeting.

Many children with high anxiety lack close friends, which is sometimes due to shyness and low self-confidence. In addition, many families simply have not facilitated regular playdates for their children. Playing with friends provides an unparalleled opportunity to develop social skills and to overcome shyness and social anxiety. Developing closer peer relationships can also provide children with a new role that can replace less positive roles and self-perceptions. Making friends can enhance self-esteem while integrating children back into a normalized trajectory of social development. A key strategy to help children make and keep close friends is to repeatedly arrange successful playdates with peers who the child likes (or might like) and provide clear guidelines for them in terms of acting as a good host.

☛ **Therapist Note:** Although the term *playdate* is often not appropriate for children over the age of 10 years, the principles of this session still apply to early adolescents (up to age 13). Try replacing playdate terminology with "get-togethers" or "having friends over" when talking with the family.

GOALS

1. Teach the parents the importance of developing regular playdates as a way for children to find a new role, feel more included by peers at school, and overcome shyness and anxiety.
2. Teach the parents how to identify potential friends for playdates.
3. Teach the family key skills for hosting successful playdates.

PREPARATION AND MATERIALS

- The therapist and parents will find the parenting book *Good Friends Are Hard to Find* (Frankel, 1996) useful to understand the practicalities of finding potential playmates (see the "Using Organized Activities to Find Friends" chapter) and arranging and hosting playdates successfully (the "Using the Telephone to Make Closer Friends" and "Having Fun Playdates" chapters). Although the current session and its handout cover these areas as well, the additional insights in these chapters are helpful. Parents may wish to get a copy of this book.
- Photocopy the Making Friends Checklist and the Playdate Record Sheet.

SESSION

With Child; Parents Optional (50% of the Session)

Introduce the concept of having a friend over to play at the child's house.

If appropriate, provide the rationale for having playdates with peers: The child can develop more or better friendships, overcome shyness, and have fun.

Ask rhetorically whether other children (1) want to come to a playdate where the host is bossy and chooses all the games (and plays them); or (2) whether they want to come to a playdate where the host is friendly, lets the guest choose what games to play, and makes it fun for them.

☞ **Therapist Note:** This point could be exemplified by two cartoon-based stories ("which would be a more fun play-date" would be the eventual question). These could be sketched out quickly with stick figures.

Suggest that the point of a playdate is to make closer friends with children that we like. We need to help children who come to our house to have a good time so that they want to be our friend too, and so they want to come back again.

Ask the child for information about peers he or she might want to invite to play. (*"Who would be on a list like that?" "Who would be on the top of a list like that?"*)

☞ **Therapist Note:** Although much of this session will seem very self-evident to the typically developing child, these insights and skills on friendships can be novel to children with high anxiety. Do not be afraid to correct distorted and erroneous conceptions about the nature of friendship and related social skills that may come up in this session.

Teach the child how good friends host a playdate.

The guest should choose all the games throughout the entire playdate.

We want to make sure our friend has fun. So, do you think that it is a good idea for us to choose the games when a friend comes over, or is it a better idea to let our friend choose all the games?

Always stay with the guest. It is never acceptable to go off and play by oneself when a guest is over, even if the guest wants to play a less-desired game. Play only with the guest and don't leave the guest alone.

Okay, so the two main rules we know about having a play-date are (1) the guest gets to choose all the games we play; and (2) always stay with the guest, and make sure I am playing with him or her! This helps my friend have a lot of fun and want to come back!

Give compliments. The host should praise the guest by giving compliments, saying "nice try," and so on. The child should not criticize the guest or the types of things that the guest wants to do.

With Parents; Child Optional (50% of the Session)

Inquire about the family's completion of Challenge homework.

Depending on what session was conducted in the previous week, Challenge homework assignments will vary. In CBT, it is always important to check on the family's completion of the homework, the corresponding rewards for the child, and any problems that may have arisen during the tasks that were assigned.

Introduce the purpose of the module.

Remind the parents that it is important to give children new roles so that they can begin to view themselves in more positive ways. This week the topic is finding ways to help the child develop closer relationships with friends.

Describe the rationale for helping children develop and maintain friendships.

Explain that close friendships teach important social skills that will make relationships in school, work, family, and personal life more rewarding and successful.

Suggest that when children who like each other spend time together in a playdate, they get to know each other and find enjoyable activities to do together, which helps build friendship. Repeated playdates help children become close friends and during playdate activities they often learn to trust each other. This provides the children with a valuable form of peer support that can help foster the development of a positive self-image (i.e., as someone who is accepted and valued).

Ask the parents how many friends their child has regular playdates with.

Inquire as to what the playdates are like and how frequent they are.

For children who have few friends, help the parents brainstorm sources of new friends.

Mention that there are generally three main sources of friends: school, the neighborhood, and extracurricular activities. There are two basic steps to yielding playdates from these sources: (1) Ask which children your child likes in each setting, and (2) observe the setting and see who your child interacts with. Once a potential playmate is identified, ask if your child likes the peer enough to ask her or him over. If the child identifies a potential playmate, parents can attempt to arrange for a playdate using the approach described below.

For children who have few friends, review extracurricular activities as a potential source of friends.

Ask what extracurricular activities the child participates in. Provide feedback that it is ideal for the child to be involved in one or two extracurricular activities with children of the same age who live close enough to the child to come over without much inconvenience.

Suggest sports, arts and crafts, or Scouting (close to the child's house) as good places to make playdate contacts. Help troubleshoot possible extracurricular activities for the child.

Note that more than two extracurricular activities make children quite busy, and their free time might be better spent in one-on-one playdates where closer friendships can be developed.

For all children, help parents plan for successful playdates with new or existing friends.

Explain that even if the child currently has some friends, the quality of these friendships could be enhanced further by examining the child's typical playdate routine. If the child does not have many friends, playdates are important for the child's friendship development.

Present the Making Friends Checklist to the parents. Review the suggestions for successful playdates with the parents and discuss in greater depth the skills or techniques that they do not currently use.

Discuss the feasibility of a regular playdate schedule for the child.

Troubleshoot with the parents on how one supervised playdate of 1 to 2 hours could be arranged this week. How might the parents alter their schedule to make it feasible (weekend playdates are sometimes easiest in big cities)? How might the child's schedule be altered to make it feasible (e.g., reducing weekend TV watching)?

If the parents comment on the amount of work involved in this, remind them that a major time commitment is often required early on to help children develop the skills and resources they need to reduce their anxiety. Remind the parents of the importance of playdates.

Review the playdate homework assignment with the family.

Using the child's suggestions of preferred candidates for playdates as a starting point, discuss how a playdate might be arranged with a peer who has not come over before, or at least not recently.

The parents should remember that a short playdate of 1 to 2 hours is best for the initial get-togethers.

It is important that the child act as the host at least initially, and that the playdate be at home rather than at a public location (e.g., museum, beach) if at all possible. True friendship is usually born out of enjoyable interactions in day-to-day settings in which casual conversations, a low-key pace, and the freedom to choose from various activities are possible. When caregivers are able to provide minimal input and allow children to get to know each other. There is a greater likelihood of true camaraderie developing. The home environment is ideally suited to these requirements.

HANDOUT

Making Friends Checklist

Children with close friends feel more confident and accepted. Being a good friend is a positive role that helps children feel good about themselves. Parents of school-age children can help. Review the following suggestions about get-togethers and playdates and consider strategies that you have not tried yet.

You should usually:

Host some of the playdates, in order to have more control over how they turn out.

_____Ensure that the guest suggests at least one activity to do before the playdate occurs.

Keep playdates short (1–2 hours) early in a friendship, so boredom and bad feelings are prevented.

_____Ensure that siblings are busy so they don't join in the playdate. It is important that most playdates remain one-on-one.

Clean up and set up the place where the agreed-upon play activity will happen (such as a clear spot on the bedroom floor for a board game).

_____Make TV and video games off-limits (or save the last 30 minutes for TV or video games to use as an incentive).

Make yourselves available to intervene if there is a problem or the children get bored, but otherwise let the children play by themselves.

_____Check with your child on how playdates go. The feedback will help determine if it is worth it to try another playdate with the same child.

HANDOUT

Playdate Record Sheet

When your child has a get-together or playdate, record how it was set up and how it went. This week, take notes on the outcome of one get-together.

EXAMPLE
I helped my child identify a friend by: Noticing my son talking to a boy named Brian in his karate class. I asked him if he'd like to invite Brian over and he agreed.

The activity my child arranged in advance to do with the guest was: Play *Monopoly*.

This is what happened during the playdate: They played *Monopoly* for an hour and seemed to have fun. I gave them a snack, and I took Brian home.

PLAYDATE NOTES

Date and place of playdate: _____

I helped my child identify a friend by: _____

_____

_____

The activity my child arranged in advance to do with the guest was: _____

_____

This is what happened during the playdate: _____

_____

_____

_____

FINAL SESSION

Termination

BACKGROUND

The goal of the termination session is to help children feel good about their accomplishments and to plan for the future. The therapist should emphasize that treatment gains will be maintained if the family continues to use the communication and exposure techniques emphasized in this program.

Although the CBT model does not emphasize the therapist-client relationship as a key curative factor, the alliance is always important in any therapy, and the child's bond with the therapist can be very intense in CBT due to the exposure elements (i.e., having gone through a lot of emotional times together). It is important not to underestimate this connection or to shy away from it at the end. The family will benefit from a sense of closure—even if just partial (e.g., because there are plans for a checkup session or the possible need for later assistance has been raised). This generally comes from a combination of positive reflection on the family's progress and an honest sharing of feelings about ending treatment from all parties.

GOALS

1. Help the child and parents develop a positive attitude about their progress in the program.
2. Review skills learned in the program and plan for the future.
3. Discuss termination issues.

PREPARATION AND MATERIALS

- Prepare any party materials (e.g., snacks), certificate, card, or small gift for the child. For most children, a certificate of

completion printed from a free Internet site and tailored to one of their interests (e.g., with a cartoon of a horse for an equestrienne), a small assortment of treats (e.g., some cookies, chips, soda), or a small gift are sufficient.
- Photocopy and bring the Planning for the Future handout.

SESSION

With Child Alone (50% of the Session)

Welcome the child to the final session and initiate the party or ritual.

Explain that in this session, the main goal is to talk about how the child has done in the program, and have a small celebration (or equivalent ritual, such as gift-giving).

Present snacks, certificates, and so on to the child and compliment him or her for effort in the program.

Review the child's progress in the program, including focus on positive accomplishments and solicitation of the child's self-perceptions of progress.

Address termination issues with the child.

Discuss termination issues from the therapist's perspective. It is helpful to note that it has been a pleasure to work with the child; it is normal to miss people you like when you can't see them anymore; and that the therapist will miss working with the child.

Ask how the child feels about ending the program, and ask her or him to name one good thing and one bad thing about the program being over. Empathize as appropriate, and reflect positively on the child's pleasure at finishing the program.

I know what you mean about being glad you have your Tuesdays free again! You've worked really hard coming here every Tuesday for 16 weeks—I bet you've got a ton of other things you could be doing like playing with your new friends in the neighborhood!

The child is free to disclose feelings or not during this conversation—there is no benefit to pressing the child on this.

Encourage the child to continue to use the KICK plan anytime he or she feels nervous.

Review the importance of continuing to use the KICK plan in situations that make the child feel nervous. Note that everyone becomes nervous from time to time, and only some people are lucky enough to know how to deal with these feelings. Point out that the KICK plan is something from the therapist that the child can keep forever and always use to feel better when he or she gets scared. Remind the child that the therapist also uses coping skills to deal with anxiety—they can help everyone.

With Parents; Child Optional (25% of the Session)

Review the child's progress and the family's role in the intervention.

Congratulate the parents on their dedication and involvement in the program (as appropriate).

Ask about the parents' reactions to ending the program.

Provide a brief assessment of the child's strengths and areas that may need further work.

Present the Planning for the Future handout. Emphasize that the child will probably continue to have periodic difficulties with anxiety in the future. Therefore, continued parental vigilance for cues of anxious child behavior will help the parents understand that new maladaptive behaviors exhibited by the child in some situations may in fact reflect anxiety.

For instance, a child who resists attending a new after-school program because it is "stupid" may actually be experiencing anxiety about some aspect of the program.

Point out that it is easy for children with anxiety to view themselves (and be viewed by others) as passive or shy. Helping children see themselves in a new light (e.g., "brave") and, from the parents' perspective, learning to think about children in more positive terms ("sometimes sensitive, but often courageous") will help them find alternate roles in the world rather than being anxious children.

With Parents and Child Together (25% of the Session)

Briefly review the past week's Challenge tasks.

Focus on any positives from the exposure assignments and give the child praise for effort.

Review progress with the parents and child together.

If the child has made significant progress in some areas of anxiety, explain that it can be helpful to evaluate if there are still areas to work on by briefly rating fears of the original hierarchy items. Read several of the key fears that have improved from the original hierarchy and ask the parents and child to rate these situations again with the Feelings Thermometer. Do not disclose the child's original ratings prior to obtaining the new ratings.

If the child has several items that are currently rated lower than they were at the start of the program, provide this information to the family and emphasize the child's progress in reducing anxiety.

Wow, before the program, you rated "Keeping my room messy all day" as a 9! Now you rated it as a 1! Wow, that's a big change—you really got over that fear!

If the child has made minimal improvement on the Feelings Thermometer according to the new ratings, but the family views the child as having made improvements, reiterate the family's sense of improvement, but do not draw attention to the lack of improvement on the numerical ratings, which may not accurately reflect the child's progress.

Congratulate the family on hard work, reiterate any key ongoing goals for the family, and end the session.

Planning for the Future

Congratulations! Your family has completed the Building Confidence Program. Be sure to give yourself a pat on the back for all of your effort! It is important to make plans to continue helping your child cope with anxiety. Here are some ideas to keep in mind:

1. **Negotiate with your child to keep facing any new fears and provide rewards for effort, just like we did in this program.**

   Identify situations, activities, or thoughts that frighten your child. Then set up a list of increasing exposures to these situations, all the way up to completely facing the fears.

   Reward your child for each step completed as he or she faces fears.

2. **Find ways to free your child from the role of being an anxious child.**

   Search for and point out times when your child acts courageously.

   Make an effort to think of your child's behavior in new ways. For instance, rather than thinking of a child as shy, try to find the positives, such as, "She's a very considerate child who also values time by herself."

3. **Use communication skills with your child.**

   When your child is feeling anxious or angry, avoid giving reassurance, giving advice, or criticizing. Label your child's feelings and wait *calmly* while your child copes with those feelings.

When you have a disagreement with your child, use problem solving. Listen to your child's side of the story without interrupting. State your side briefly. Think of all possible solutions. Decide together which solutions to try.

4. **Make sure that your child continues to develop self-help skills. This builds confidence and self-esteem.**

   Ask yourself: Is my child as independent as the other children?

   For instance, are the other children dressing themselves, walking home by themselves, being responsible for their own room?

   If your child is less independent, perhaps it is time to encourage your child catch up so he or she continues to feel competent and confident.

5. **Encourage your child to develop and maintain friendships.**

   Children with good friends have higher self-esteem and fewer anxiety problems.

   Weekly playdates are an essential part of developing and keeping close friends. Remember, parents should play an active role in encouraging playdates.

Examples of Exposures Conducted
With 6- to 13-Year-Old Clients

• •

Category	Target Anxious Behavior
Separating from parents	Spending 1 to 15 minutes alone in a public place (e.g., store), with Mom out of eyesight (increase the time slowly with each trial of the exposure).
	Playing with toys in my room, with Mom in the next room (vary: door open, door closed).
	Playing with toys in my room, with Mom and Dad downstairs (vary: door open, door closed).
	Playing with toys by myself for 15 minutes, not knowing where Mom is in the house.
	Spending 1 to 30 minutes (increase the time slowly) alone in a room with nothing to do (vary: lights on, lights off) (can be done in session therapy and at home).

Category	Target Anxious Behavior
	Mom picking me up late from school or other social events, 1 to 10 minutes (increase the time slowly); work up to not knowing when Mom will pick me up.
	Staying in the house while Mom steps outside briefly (e.g., watering plants) without checking through my windows.
	Staying home with a babysitter while Mom is out for 30 minutes to 4 hours (increase the time slowly each occasion; can begin with Mom elsewhere in the house).
	Not asking to call Mom from aide's phone during school days (can begin with one or two exceptions per day).
	Going on a playdate at a friend's house; Mom doesn't stay (can begin with Mom staying most of the time and leaving only for 5 to 10 minutes for a walk around the block; increase the time away from Mom on future playdates).
	Not calling Mom during a playdate at a friend's house (can begin with one or two exceptions per playdate).
	Going on a sleepover at a friend's house. (Write a contract that everyone signs stating that the child will only come home in an emergency, not just because he or she is anxious; allow one or two phone calls before 8 P.M.).
	Staying home with big sister or Grandma while Mom is out, not asking when Mom is coming home, not waiting up for her (slowly increase the time Mom is out).
	Staying home with Dad while Mom is out, not asking Dad questions about Mom's return the entire time (can begin with one or two exceptions per time; increase the time slowly for Mom's absence).

Category	Target Anxious Behavior
	Walking in a public place without holding onto Mom's hand.
	Going to Grandma's without bags of security items (including two blankets plus all toys).
	Staying at Grandma's with only one call to parents.
	Staying at Grandma's the entire time without calling parents.
	Imagining Mom and Dad in a car accident and telling a story about it (later: change image and story to a happy or silly ending— e.g., everyone was worried it was a bad accident, but it turned out to be a broken taillight).
Fear of the dark	Staying outside calmly (not rushing home) after it has turned visibly dark.
	Staying with Mom in the yard at sundown with an enjoyable activity for 20 minutes, watching the sun set (with and without the dog).
	Staying calmly at home without checking the lights around the house.
	Spending 1 minute alone in an empty closet (can be done in therapy and at home).
	Leaving the house and going on a field trip at night (e.g., to a restaurant).
	Imagining scary sounds around my house at night when everyone's asleep, typing up a short story on my laptop about what it sounds like (burglars), get an image of the story in my head; then change the story and image to a happy ending (e.g., just the wind, pipes, or trees making noise).

Category	Target Anxious Behavior
Bedtime routine	Going to sleep with the desk lamp only (overhead light must be off).
	Going to sleep with a night-light only (desk lamp and overhead light off).
	Going to sleep by myself after a brief goodnight hug and kiss from Dad (Dad can stay 1 to 10 minutes).
	Going to sleep by myself after a brief goodnight from Dad; Dad doesn't stay (and sleeps elsewhere).
	Mom sitting next to bed for 15 minutes at bedtime (slowly reduce this to 0 minutes).
	Sleeping without Mom in the room (vary: door open, door closed).
	Staying in my own bed after a nightmare, and not calling out to Mom and Dad.
	Going to bed without locking the doors and smelling Mom's perfume (to ensure Mom is not leaving).
	Sleeping on my own bed in the same room with my brothers.
	Sleeping alone in own bed and new room without my brothers.
Social anxiety: phone	Answering one phone call per day and summoning the person for whom the call is intended.
	Talking to a familiar adult on the phone (in-session version: talking to the therapist in the next room).
	Talking to a familiar friend on the phone (e.g., to ask for homework assignment).
	Talking to a new friend on the phone (e.g., to ask for homework assignment; talk about movies; ask over for a playdate).

Category	Target Anxious Behavior
Social anxiety: same-age peers	Asking to play with new friends at recess (slowly increase the time from 2 minutes to the entire period).
	Joining a conversation with a new friend (find out at least two things that he or she likes). Saying hi to a group of kids on the playground.
	Sitting next to a target peer at lunch (increased difficulty: ask two or three questions about the peer's interests).
	Lining up with a friend at school in the hallway. (Teacher doesn't count as a friend!)
	Greeting a target peer upon arriving at school in the morning.
	Inviting a new friend to get together in person.
	Saying hello to a group of same-age peers at Sunday school.
	Joining a conversation with less well-known same-age peers at Sunday school.
	Initiating a conversation with a less well-known same-age peers at Sunday school.
	Joining a play activity in the schoolyard in the morning without hanging onto Mom.
	Asking a new friend for help.
Social anxiety: looking incompetent	Doing something silly in public like dropping papers all over the floor or falling down (usually done in therapy).
	Asking for directions from confederates and strangers around the office (done in session with the therapist).

Category	Target Anxious Behavior
	Running office errands (e.g., borrowing pencils) in which I go up to people and knock on doors (in therapy).
	Eating in front of therapist and (later) confederates (can be done in session).
	Eating (and making a mess) in a cafeteria or public place with many strangers around.
Social anxiety: performance	Reading aloud in front of family members or relatives (begin with short readings and small audience, and slowly increase).
	Reading aloud in front of strangers or progressively larger group (in session: ask any available staff or colleagues to serve as confederates).
	Reading aloud to varying groups, intentionally making mistakes on 1 to 10 words (slowly increase errors).
	Making an oral presentation about a preferred topic in front of family or new adults.
	Running laps or doing sit-ups/gym exercises in front of other people (increased difficulty: run slowly, or do exercises awkwardly on purpose).
	Playing a song on guitar in front of progressively larger group.
	Singing (standing up) in front of therapist and Mom (in session).
	Asking for directions around the therapy office from strangers, with further need of clarification (i.e., pretend to not understand what they say the first time or two).
Social anxiety: school	Raising my hand and answering a question in class each day (increased level of difficulty: two to three questions per day).

Category	Target Anxious Behavior
	Asking the teacher for help on a problem in class each day.
	Mom dropping me off late at school, 1 to 10 minutes (slowly increase the time; do this once or twice per week).
	Meeting new adults (teachers?) and asking them questions (interview them).
	Writing on a chalkboard or whiteboard in front of others (in-session version: recruit people from the office, such as the secretary, assistants, and the child's parents, and use them as the audience.)
Social anxiety: laughing, teasing	Listening to a tape of people laughing. (The point is to desensitize to laughter and develop calm thoughts that "people aren't always laughing at me.")
	Sitting next to a few confederates who are laughing and joking with each other. (Calm thought: "They are not laughing at me; they just told a funny joke.")
	Being in close proximity to children who are laughing and joking with each other (e.g., on a playground).
	Reading at normal speed in front of therapist and Mom.
	Reading at normal speed in front of a few unfamiliar people.
	Imagining being teased about my hair and appearance by mean kids (like Joe) and new kids I just met at Sunday school. (Then, change this mental image to something pleasant, like the children inviting me to play.)
Homework worries	Starting homework within an hour of getting home from school (then within a half hour).
	Starting homework with one reminder from Mom after school.

Category	Target Anxious Behavior
	Starting homework by self with a timer after school.
	Doing homework with Mom standing by to provide help as needed (just short of maximum support).
	Doing homework with Mom in the room to answer 10 questions, then 5 questions, then no questions (slowly decrease the number).
	Doing homework by myself with Mom checking in every so often.
	Doing homework by myself the entire time.
	Doing homework for 30 minutes before taking a break or doing any fun stuff.
	Completing daily homework assignments in one seating without taking breaks or doing any fun stuff in between.
	Doing homework without complaints or self-defeating remarks.
	Add these elements to the exposure task incrementally: (1) starting homework on time; (2) starting homework by myself; (3) doing homework without complaining; (4) doing homework without Mom's help.
Disaster and news worries	Imagining a fire in your house, then typing up a short narrative on laptop (later: change image and story to a happy or silly ending).
	Imagining bad weather (e.g., storms), then drawing a picture about it (later: change image and picture to a happy or silly ending).
	Looking through magazines depicting natural disasters or world events, then drawing pictures about them (later: change pictures to happy or silly endings).

Category	Target Anxious Behavior
	Watching the news or reading about the war, natural disasters, or troubling news about the state of the world, then typing or drawing a picture of the scariest image about these stories. Change the picture to have a happier ending (e.g., the war ends, bullets turn to water, punches turn to high-fives).
Appearance worries	Spending less and less time (less than 15 minutes; 5 to 9 minutes; less than 5 minutes) styling hair in the morning.
	Going swimming without a T-shirt on (to address the fear that others would say the child is fat).
	Obtaining attractiveness ratings from others of pictures depicting children with and without defined cleft chins and flat hair (to show that people generally don't think there's anything wrong or unattractive about kids with clefts or hair that doesn't spike—these kids can in fact be rather attractive).
	Drawing a picture of a shorter kid being teased by a tall kid; then changing the picture so it has a happy ending.
	Role playing a tall kid–short kid teasing scenario and reversing roles with therapist (in session).
	Listening to a tape of people laughing, imagining that they're making fun of me because I'm small (then, change the scenario so I am wrong and they were just laughing at a good joke).
	Practicing keeping my cool and using sarcasm with adult confederates who are laughing at my small size.
Perfectionism	Drawing a picture with dot marker for the therapist with my eyes closed and showing it to Mom. Hang it up on the therapist's wall ("so the other kids can see it").

Category	Target Anxious Behavior
	At home, wear a silly hairstyle, from after school until bedtime (can begin with shorter length of time; vary by having the child wear the hairstyle in public).
	Messing up on one of my masterpiece drawings on purpose, using the nondominant hand.
	Playing a game and losing on purpose (point: not being the best at everything; the fun is in playing with someone, not winning).
	Playing a piece on the clarinet and messing up on purpose (vary the type of audience to make it more or less challenging).
	Not asking others, "Was I good?" for the entire day (can begin with one or two exceptions per day).
Other worries	Borrowing something from an adult confederate (e.g., a pencil), "accidentally" breaking it, and returning it with an appropriate explanation and calm attitude.
	Saying "no" to somebody, for instance, not letting them borrow something that you own.
	Not asking about Mom's and my own health (and heart problems; can begin with one or two exceptions per day).
	Imagining health problems in myself and family members (later: change story to a happy or silly ending, such as the child realizing that there is an easy cure for the problem, or that the problem is not really dangerous and turned out to be a humorous malady, like the hiccups).
	Imagining getting in trouble at school (later: change story and image to a happy or silly ending, such as the principal realizing that it was another student who caused the problem).

Category	Target Anxious Behavior
OCD: hoarding	Placing juice boxes, rocks, and toilet paper tubes in a junk box for one week (instead of storing these in my backpack and a secret place in the bathroom).
	Moving the box of junk into the carport.
	Moving the box of junk into the trash can (not throwing it out initially; getting used to it being in the trash can at home).
	Bringing hoarded items into the therapy session to discard. (Calm thought: "Someone else can use them for an art project.")
	Throwing away some items from my designer collection (e.g., useless items that have been given a special label).
OCD: compulsions, germs	Running hands all over a table that others have touched, without washing (in therapy and at home; gradually increase the amount of delay until washing from 1 to 20 minutes).
	Running hands along the sides of a trash can, without washing for 1 to 10 minutes (in therapy and at home; gradually increase the amount of delay until washing).
	Running hands all over a dry erase board (with leftover marks), without washing for 1 to 20 minutes (in therapy and at home; gradually increase the amount of delay until washing).
	Touching the toilet seat without washing for 1 to 10 minutes (in therapy and at home; gradually increase the amount of delay until washing).
	Sitting with jelly (or something else gooey) on my hands for 1 to 10 minutes without washing (in therapy and at home; gradually increase the amount of delay until washing).

Category	Target Anxious Behavior
	Leaving the room with a bottle of water (cap open) on the table, then returning a few minutes later and drinking out of the same bottle (in therapy and at home).
	Reusing the same Dixie cup when rinsing mouth (instead of using three different cups).
	Walking on the sand at the beach for 1 to 10 minutes without washing feet. (Calm thought: "I've never had sand crabs or fire ants crawl on me there!")
	Doing the dishes (that contained spaghetti or nonpreferred foods).
OCD: compulsions, stuffed animal	Refraining from performing rituals with stuffed animals one day per week.
	Refraining from performing stuffed animal rituals the entire weekend.
	Bringing stuffed animals to session and refraining from performing the rituals.
Phobias	Looking through illustrations of scary monster book, 1 to 5 minutes per picture (in session and at home; vary how close the child is to the book).
	Therapist or parent reading me the story of the scary monster book.
	Me reading the scary monster story aloud to my mom or my therapist.
	Singing the scary monster song out loud.
	Drawing the scary monster, crossing it out, then balling it up and throwing it in the trash.

Category	Target Anxious Behavior
	Imagining the scary monster's face and the song that goes with it, with eyes closed (later, change the image to a pleasant face and imagine playing a fun game with the nice person).
OCD: rituals and routines	Applying deodorant after my shirt is on and my hair has been styled.
	Leaving marks on the whiteboard without erasing them.
	Allowing Mom to change the way the blankets are arranged (e.g., pulling them down midway instead of to the end of the bed).
	Leaving several security items with the therapist for safekeeping.
	Letting my Mom take one of my favorite things for one day and not tell me where it is.
	Letting my mom take one of my favorite things and not know when it will be coming back.
OCD: repetitive topics	Not talking about *Star Wars* for a 1-hour period per day when I am around my family (slowly increase this time to the full day).
	Not asking "Am I John Doe" for a 1-hour period per day (slowly increase the length of time per day).

References

American Psychiatric Association. (1994). *Diagnostic and statistical manual of mental disorders* (4th ed.). Washington, DC: Author.

Anastasi, A. (1988). *Psychological testing* (6th ed.). New York: Macmillan Publishing Co.

Angold, A., Costello, E. J., & Erkanli, A. (1999). Comorbidity. *Journal of Child Psychology and Psychiatry, 40,* 57–87.

Bandura, A. (1986). The explanatory and predictive scope of self-efficacy theory. *Journal of Social and Clinical Psychology, 4,* 359–373.

Bandura, A. (1997). *Self-efficacy: The exercise of control.* New York: Freeman.

Barlow, D. H., Brown, T. A., & Craske, M. G. (1994). Definitions of panic attacks and panic disorder in the DSM-IV: Implications for research. *Journal of Abnormal Psychology, 103,* 553–564.

Barrett, P. M. (1998). Group therapy for childhood anxiety disorders. *Journal of Clinical Child Psychology, 27,* 459–468.

Barrett, P. M., Dadds, M. R., & Rapee, R. M. (1996). Family treatment of childhood anxiety: A controlled trial. *Journal of Consulting and Clinical Psychology, 64,* 333–342.

Barrett, P. M., Duffy, A. L., Dadds, M. R., & Rapee, R. M. (2001). Cognitive-behavioral treatment of anxiety disorders in children: Long-term (6-year) follow-up. *Journal of Consulting and Clinical Psychology, 69*, 135–141.

Barrett, P. M., & Shortt, A. L. (2003). Parental involvement in the treatment of anxious children. In A. E. Kazdin & J. R. Weisz (Eds.), *Evidence-based psychotherapies for children and adolescents* (pp. 101–119). New York: Guilford.

Beck, A. T. (1976). *Cognitive therapy and the emotional disorders.* Oxford, England: International Universities Press.

Beck, A. T., Rush, A. J., Shaw, B. F., & Emery, G. (1979). *Cognitive therapy for depression.* Hoboken, NJ: Wiley.

Beidel, D. C., Fink, C. M., & Turner, S. M. (1996). Stability of anxious symptomatology in children. *Journal of Abnormal Child Psychology, 24*, 257–269.

Beidel, D. C., Turner, S. M., & Morris, T. L. (1999). Psychopathology of childhood social phobia. *Journal of the American Academy of Child and Adolescent Psychiatry, 38*, 643–650.

Bell-Dolan, D., & Brazeal, T. J. (1993). Separation anxiety disorder, overanxious disorder, and school refusal. *Child and Adolescent Psychiatric Clinics of North America, 2*, 563–580.

Berg, C. Z., Rapoport, J. L., Whitaker, A., Davies, M., Leonard, H., Swedo, S. E., et al. (1989). Childhood obsessive compulsive disorder: A two-year prospective follow-up of a community sample. *Journal of the American Academy of Child and Adolescent Psychiatry, 28*, 528–533.

Berger, C., & Donnadieu, S. (2006). Categorization by schema relations and perceptual similarity in 5–year-olds and adults: A study in vision and in audition. *Journal of Experimental Child Psychology, 93*, 304–321.

Bergman, R. L., Piacentini, J., & McCracken, J. T. (2002). Prevalence and description of selective mutism in a school-based sample. *Journal of the American Academy of Child and Adolescent Psychiatry, 41*, 938–946.

Birmaher, B., Khetarpal, S., Brent, D., & Cully, M. (1997). The Screen for Child Anxiety Related Emotional Disorders (SCARED): Scale construction and psychometric characteristics. *Journal of the American Academy of Child and Adolescent Psychiatry, 36,* 545–553.

Birmaher, B., & Ollendick, T. H. (2004). Childhood-onset panic disorder. In T. H. Ollendick & J. S. March (Eds.), *Phobic and anxiety disorders in children and adolescents: A clinician's guide to effective psychosocial and pharmacological interventions* (pp. 306–333). New York: Oxford University Press.

Blagg, N. R., & Yule, W. (1984). The behavioural treatment of school refusal: A comparative study. *Behaviour Research and Therapy, 22,* 119–127.

Borkovec, T. D., & Inz, J. (1990). The nature of worry in generalized anxiety disorder: A predominance of thought activity. *Behaviour Research and Therapy, 28,* 153–158.

Bowen, R. C., Offord, D. R., & Boyle, M. H. (1990). The prevalence of overanxious disorder and separation anxiety disorder: Results from the Ontario Child Health Study. *Journal of the American Academy of Child and Adolescent Psychiatry, 29,* 753–758.

Brewin, C. R. (2006). Understanding cognitive behaviour therapy: A retrieval competition account. *Behaviour Research and Therapy, 44,* 765–784.

Briggs-Gowan, M. J., Horwitz, S. M., Schwab-Stone, M. E., Leventhal, J. M., & Leaf, P. J. (2000). Mental health in pediatric settings: Distribution of disorders and factors related to service use. *Journal of the American Academy of Child and Adolescent Psychiatry, 39,* 841–849.

Brown, T. A., Chorpita, B. F., & Barlow, D. H. (1998). Structural relationships among dimensions of the DSM-IV anxiety and mood disorders and dimensions of negative affect, positive affect, and autonomic arousal. *Journal of Abnormal Psychology, 107,* 179–192.

Cantwell, D. P., & Baker, L. (1989). Stability and natural history of DSM-III childhood diagnoses. *Journal of the American Academy of Child and Adolescent Psychiatry, 28,* 691–700.

Capps, L., & Ochs, E. (1995). Out of place: Narrative insights into agoraphobia. *Discourse Processes, 19,* 407–439.

Carlson, V. J., & Harwood, R. L. (2003). Alternate pathways to competence: Culture and early attachment relationships. In S. M. Johnson & V. E. Whiffen (Eds.), *Attachment processes in couple and family therapy* (pp. 85–99). New York: Guilford.

Carver, L. J., & Vaccaro, B. G. (2007). 12–month-old infants allocate increased neural resources to stimuli associated with negative adult emotion. *Developmental Psychology, 43,* 54–69.

Chorpita, B. F., & Barlow, D. H. (1998). The development of anxiety: The role of control in the early environment. *Psychological Bulletin, 124,* 3–21.

Cicchetti, D. V., & Toth, S. L. (1998). The development of depression in children and adolescents. *American Psychologist, 53,* 221–241.

Cobham, V. E., Dadds, M. R., & Spence, S. H. (1998). The role of parental anxiety in the treatment of childhood anxiety. *Journal of Consulting and Clinical Psychology, 66,* 893–905.

Cohen, J. A., Deblinger, E., Mannarino, A. P., & Steer, R. A. (2004). A multisite, randomized controlled trial for children with sexual abuse-related PTSD symptoms. *Journal of the American Academy of Child and Adolescent Psychiatry, 43,* 393–402.

Cortes, A. M., Saltzman, K. M., Weems, C. F., Regnault, H. P., Reiss, A. L., & Carrion, V. G. (2005). Development of anxiety disorders in a traumatized pediatric population: A preliminary longitudinal evaluation. *Child Abuse and Neglect, 29,* 905–914.

Costello, E. J. (1989). Child psychiatric disorders and their correlates: a primary care pediatric sample. *Journal of the American Academy of Child and Adolescent Psychiatry, 28,* 851–855.

Craske, M. G. (1999). *Anxiety disorders: Psychological approaches to theory and treatment.* Boulder, CO: Westview Press.

Dadds, M. R., James, R. C., Barrett, P. M., & Verhulst, F. C. (2004). Diagnostic issues. In T. H. Ollendick & J. S. March (Eds.), *Phobic and anxiety disorders in children and adolescents* (pp. 3–33). New York: Oxford University Press.

Dadds, M. R., Spence, S. H., Holland, D. E., Barrett, P. M., & Laurens, K. R. (1997). Prevention and early intervention for anxiety disorders: A controlled trial. *Journal of Consulting and Clinical Psychology, 65,* 627–635.

Egeland, B., Pianta, R., & O'Brien, M. A. (1993). Maternal intrusiveness in infancy and child maladaptation in early school years. *Development and Psychopathology, 5,* 359–370.

Eisenberg, N., Fabes, R. A., Damon, W., & Eisenberg, N. (1998). Prosocial development. In D. William & R. M. Lerner (Eds.), *Handbook of child psychology, Vol 3. Social, emotional, and personality development* (5th ed., pp. 701–778). Hoboken, NJ: Wiley.

Ekman, P. (1992). Arc there basic emotions? *Psychological Review, 99,* 550–553.

Eley, T. C. (2001). Contributions of behavioral genetics research: Quantifying genetic, shared environmental and nonshared environmental influences. In M. W. Vasey & M. R. Dadds (Eds.), *The developmental psychopathology of anxiety* (pp. 45–59). New York: Oxford University Press.

Faber, A., & Maslich, E. (2001). *How to talk so kids will listen and listen so kids will talk.* New York: Avon.

Fanselow, M. S. (1994). Neural organization of the defensive behavior system responsible for fear. *Psychonomic Bulletin and Review, 1,* 429–438.

Fiske, S. T., & Taylor, S. E. (1991). *Social cognition* (2nd ed.). McGraw-Hill.

Fox, N. A., Henderson, H. A., Marshall, P. J., Nichols, K. E., & Ghera, M. M. (2005). Behavioral inhibition: Linking biology and behavior within a developmental framework. *Annual Review of Psychology, 56,* 235–262.

Franklin, M. E., Rynn, M. A., Foa, E. B., & March, J. S. (2004). Pediatric obsessive-compulsive disorder. In T. H. Ollendick & J. S. March (Eds.), *Phobic and anxiety disorders in children and adolescents: A clinician's guide to effective psychosocial and pharmacological interventions* (pp. 381–404). New York: Oxford University Press.

Frankel, F. (1996). *Good friends are hard to find.* Los Angeles, CA: Perspective Publishing.

Gottman, J. M., Katz, L. F., & Hooven, C. (1997). *Meta-emotion: How families communicate emotionally.* Hillsdale, NJ: Erlbaum.

Gullone, E. (1996). Normal fear in people with a physical or intellectual disability. *Clinical Psychology Review, 16,* 689–706.

Gunnar, M. R. (2001). The role of glucocorticoids in anxiety disorders: A critical analysis. In M. W. Vasey & M. R. Dadds (Eds.), *The developmental psychopathology of anxiety* (pp. 143–159). New York: Oxford University Press.

Henggeler, S. W., & Lee, T. (2003). Multisystemic treatment of serious clinical problems. In A. E. Kazdin & J. R. Weisz (Eds.), *Evidence-based psychotherapies for children and adolescents* (pp. 301–322). New York: Guilford.

Hudziak, J. J., Rudiger, L. P., Neale, M. C., Heath, A. C., & Todd, R. D. (2000). A twin study of inattentive, aggressive, and anxious/depressed behaviors. *Journal of the American Academy of Child and Adolescent Psychiatry, 39,* 469–476.

Hwang, W. (2006). The psychotherapy adaptation and modification framework (PAMF): Application to Asian Americans. *American Psychologist, 61,* 702–715.

Hwang, W., Wood, J. J., Lin, K., & Cheung, F. (2006). Cognitive-behavioral therapy with Chinese Americans: Research, theory, and clinical practice. *Cognitive and Behavioral Practice, 13,* 293–303.

Ispa, J. M., Fine, M. A., Halgunseth, L. C., Harper, S., Robinson, J., Boyce, L. et al. (2004). Maternal intrusiveness, maternal warmth, and mother-toddler relationship outcomes: Variations across low-income ethnic and acculturation groups. *Child Development, 75,* 1613–1631.

Izard, C. E. (1992). Basic emotions, relations among emotions, and emotion-cognition relations. *Psychological Review, 99,* 561–565.

Jensen, A. L., & Weisz, J. R. (2002). Assessing match and mismatch between practitioner-generated and standardized interview-generated diagnoses for clinic-referred children and adolescents. *Journal of Consulting and Clinical Psychology, 70,* 158–168.

Jensen-Doss, A. (2005). Evidence-based diagnosis: Incorporating diagnostic instruments into clinical practice. *Journal of the American Academy of Child and Adolescent Psychiatry, 44,* 947–952.

Jensen-Doss, A., Cook, K. T., & McLeod, B. D. (in press). Diagnostic issues. In D. Reitman (Ed.), *Handbook of assessment, conceptualization, and treatment, volume II: Children and adolescents.* Hoboken, NJ: John Wiley & Sons.

Kagan, J., Reznick, J. S., & Gibbons, J. (1989). Inhibited and uninhibited types of children. *Child Development, 60,* 838–845.

Kagan, J., Snidman, N., Zentner, M., & Peterson, E. (1999). Infant temperament and anxious symptoms in school age children. *Development and Psychopathology, 11,* 209–224.

Kaufman, J., Birmaher, B., Brent, D., Rao, U., Flynn, C., Moreci, P., et al. (1997). Schedule for affective disorders and schizophrenia for school-age children present and lifetime version (K-SADS-PL): Initial reliability and validity data. *Journal of the American Academy of Child and Adolescent Psychiatry, 36,* 980–988.

Kazdin, A. E., & Weisz, J. R. (2003). *Evidence-based psychotherapies for children and adolescents.* New York: Guilford.

Kearney, C. A. (2003). Bridging the gap among professionals who address youths with school absenteeism: Overview and suggestions for consensus. *Professional Psychology: Research and Practice, 34,* 57–65.

Kendall, P. C. (1994). Treating anxiety disorders in children: Results of a randomized clinical trial. *Journal of Consulting and Clinical Psychology, 62,* 100–110.

Kendall, P. C., Aschenbrand, S. G., & Hudson, J. L. (2003). Child-focused treatment of anxiety. In A. E. Kazdin & J. R. Weisz (Eds.), *Evidence-based psychotherapies for children and adolescents* (pp. 81–100). New York: Guilford.

Kendall, P. C., Flannery-Schroeder, E., Panichelli-Mindel, S. M., Southam-Gerow, M., Henin, A., & Warman, M. (1997). Therapy for youths with anxiety disorders: A second randomized clinical trial. *Journal of Consulting and Clinical Psychology, 65,* 366–380.

Kendall, P. C., Kane, M., Howard, B., & Siqueland, L. (1990). *Cognitive-behavioral treatment of anxious children: Treatment manual.* Ardmore, PA: Workbook Publishing.

Klein, D. N., Dougherty, L. R., & Olino, T. M. (2005). Toward guidelines for evidence-based assessment of depression in children and adolescents. *Journal of Clinical Child and Adolescent Psychology, 34,* 412–432.

Langley, A. K., Bergman, R. L., McCracken, J., & Piacentini, J. C. (2004). Impairment in childhood anxiety disorders: Preliminary examination of the Child Anxiety Impact Scale–Parent Version. *Journal of Child and Adolescent Psychopharmacology, 14,* 105–114.

Langley, A. K., Bergman, R. L., & Piacentini, J. C. (2002). Assessment of childhood anxiety. *International Review of Psychiatry, 14,* 102–113.

LeDoux, J. E. (2000). Emotion circuits in the brain. *Annual Review of Neuroscience, 23,* 155–184.

Lerda, R., Garzunel, R., & Therme, P. (1996). Analogic transfer: A strategy for adapting to spatial constraints: The case of a duel in soccer. *International Journal of Sport Psychology, 27,* 133–145.

Lewinsohn, P. M., Hops, H., Roberts, R. E., Seeley, J. R., & Andrews, J. A. (1993). Adolescent psychopathology: I. Prevalence and incidence of depression and other DSM-III-R disorders in high school students. *Journal of Abnormal Psychology, 102,* 133–144.

Ma, X. (1999). A meta-analysis of the relationship between anxiety toward mathematics and achievement in mathematics. *Journal for Research in Mathematics Education, 30,* 520–540.

Maccoby, E. E. (1992). The role of parents in the socialization of children: An historical overview. *Developmental Psychology, 28,* 1006–1017.

March, J. S. (1998). *The Multidimensional Anxiety Scale for Children (MASC).* North Tonawanda, NY: MHS.

March, J. S., Parker, J. D. A., Sullivan, K., Stallings, P., & Conners, C. K. (1997). The Multidimensional Anxiety Scale for Children (MASC): Factor structure, reliability, and validity. *Journal of the American Academy of Child and Adolescent Psychiatry, 36,* 554–565.

March, J. S., Sullivan, K., & Parker, J. (1999). Test-retest reliability of the Multidimensional Anxiety Scale for Children. *Journal of Anxiety Disorders, 13,* 349–358.

Mash, E. J., & Hunsley, J. (2005). Evidence-based assessment of child and adolescent disorders: Issues and challenges. *Journal of Clinical Child and Adolescent Psychology, 34,* 362–379.

Masi, G., Favilla, L., Millepiedi, S., & Mucci, M. (2000). Somatic symptoms in children and adolescents referred for emotional and behavioral disorders. *Psychiatry: Interpersonal and Biological Processes, 63,* 140–149.

McLeod, B. D., Wood, J. J., & Weisz, J. (2007). Examining the association between parenting and childhood anxiety: A meta-analysis. *Clinical Psychology Review, 27*, 155–172.

Mendlowitz, S. L., Manassis, K., Bradley, S., Scapillato, D., Mietzitis, S., & Shaw, B. (1999). Cognitive-behavioral group treatments in childhood anxiety disorders: The role of parental involvement. *Journal of the American Academy of Child and Adolescent Psychiatry, 38*, 1223–1229.

Minuchin, S., & Nichols, M. P. (1994). *Family healing: Strategies for hope and understanding.* New York: Simon and Schuster.

Moore, P. S., Whaley, S. E., & Sigman, M. (2004). Interaction between mothers and children: Impacts of maternal and child anxiety. *Journal of Abnormal Psychology, 113*, 471–476.

Morris, T. L. (2001). Social phobia. In M. W. Vasey & M. R. Dadds (Eds.), *The developmental psychopathology of anxiety* (pp. 435–458). New York: Oxford University Press.

Morris, T. L., & Masia, C. L. (1998). Psychometric evaluation of the Social Phobia and Anxiety Inventory for Children: Concurrent validity and normative data. *Journal of Clinical Child Psychology, 27*, 452–458.

Muris, P. (2002). Relationships between self-efficacy and symptoms of anxiety disorders and depression in a normal adolescent sample. *Personality and Individual Differences, 32*, 337–348.

Nauta, M. H., Scholing, A., Emmelkamp, P. M. G., & Minderaa, R. B. (2003). Cognitive-behavioral therapy for children with anxiety disorders in a clinical setting: No additional effect of a cognitive parent training. *Journal of the American Academy of Child and Adolescent Psychiatry, 42*, 1270–1278.

Newman, D. L., Moffitt, T. E., Caspi, A., & Magdol, L. (1996). Psychiatric disorder in a birth cohort of young adults: Prevalence, comorbidity, clinical significance, and new case incidence from ages 11–21. *Journal of Consulting and Clinical Psychology, 64*, 552–562.

Ollendick, T. H., Vasey, M. W., & King, N. J. (2001). Operant conditioning influences in childhood anxiety. In M. W. Vasey & M. R. Dadds (Eds.), *The developmental psychopathology of anxiety* (pp. 231–252). New York: Oxford University Press.

Pediatric OCD Treatment Study (POTS) Team. (2004). Cognitive-behavior therapy, sertraline, and their combination for children and adolescents with obsessive-compulsive disorder: The Pediatric OCD Treatment Study (POTS) randomized controlled trial. *Journal of the American Medical Association, 292,* 1969–1976.

Piacentini, J. C., Cohen, P., & Cohen, J. (1992). Combining discrepant diagnostic information from multiple sources: Are complex algorithms better than simple ones? *Journal of Abnormal Child Psychology, 20,* 51–63.

Piaget, J., & Inhelder, B. (1969). *The psychology of the child.* Paris: Basic Books.

Puntambekar, S., & Kolodner, J. L. (2005). Toward implementing distributed scaffolding: Helping students learn science from design. *Journal of Research in Science Teaching, 42,* 185–217.

Rachman, S. (1990). *Fear and courage* (2nd ed.). New York: Freeman.

Rapee, R. M. (2001). The developmental psychopathology of anxiety. In M. W. Vasey & M. R. Dadds (Eds.), *The developmental psychopathology of anxiety* (pp. 481–503). New York: Oxford University Press.

Redfield, R., Linton, R., & Herskovits, M. (1936). Memorandum on the study of acculturation. *American Anthropologist, 38,* 149–152.

Rubin, K. H., & Burgess, K. B. (2001). Social withdrawal and anxiety. In M. W. Vasey & M. R. Dadds (Eds.), *The developmental psychopathology of anxiety* (pp. 407–434). New York: Oxford University Press.

Rubin, K. H., Burgess, K. B., Kennedy, A. E., & Stewart, S. L. (2003). Social withdrawal in childhood. In E. J. Mash & R. A.

Barkley (Eds.), *Child psychopathology* (2nd ed., pp. 372–406). New York: Guilford.

Rumberger, R. W., & Gandara, P. (2004). Seeking equity in the education of California's English learners. *Teachers College Record, 106,* 2032–2056.

RUPP Anxiety Group. (2001). Fluvoxamine for the treatment of anxiety disorders in children and adolescents. *New England Journal of Medicine, 344,* 1279–1285.

Sattler, J. (2001). *Assessment of children: Cognitive applications.* La Mesa, CA: Author.

Schniering, C. A., Hudson, J. L., & Rapee, R. M. (2000). Issues in the diagnosis and assessment of anxiety disorders in children and adolescents. *Clinical Psychology Review, 20,* 453–478.

Schwartz, C. E., Snidman, N., & Kagan, J. (1999). Adolescent social anxiety as an outcome of inhibited temperament in childhood. *Journal of the American Academy of Child and Adolescent Psychiatry, 38,* 1008–1015.

Silove, D., & Manicavasagar, V. (2001). Early separation anxiety and its relationship to adult anxiety disorders. In M. W. Vasey & M. R. Dadds (Eds.), *The developmental psychopathology of anxiety* (pp. 459–480). New York: Oxford University Press.

Silverman, W. K., & Albano, A. M. (1996). *The Anxiety Disorders Interview Schedule for DSM-IV—Child and Parent Versions.* San Antonio, TX: Graywind.

Silverman, W. K., & Eisen, A. R. (1992). Age differences in the reliability of parent and child reports of child anxious symptomatology using a structured interview. *Journal of the American Academy of Child and Adolescent Psychiatry, 31,* 117–124.

Silverman, W. K., & Kurtines, W. M. (1996). Transfer of control: A psychosocial intervention model for internalizing disorders in youth. In E. D. Hibbs & P. S. Jensen (Eds.), *Psychosocial treatments for child and adolescent disorders: Empirically-based strategies for clinical practice* (pp. 63–81). Washington, DC: American Psychological Association.

Silverman, W. K., Kurtines, W. M., Ginsburg, G. S., Weems, C. F., Lumpkin, P. W., & Carmichael, D. H. (1999). Treating anxiety disorders in children with group cognitive-behavioral therapy: A randomized clinical trial. *Journal of Consulting and Clinical Psychology, 67,* 995–1003.

Silverman, W. K., & Ollendick, T. H. (2005). Evidence-based assessment of anxiety and its disorders in children and adolescents. *Journal of Clinical Child and Adolescent Psychology, 34,* 380–411.

Silverman, W. K., Saavedra, L. M., & Pina, A. A. (2001). Test-retest reliability of anxiety symptoms and diagnoses with Anxiety Disorders Interview Schedule for DSM-IV: Child and parent versions. *Journal of the American Academy of Child and Adolescent Psychiatry, 40,* 937–944.

Snidman, N., Kagan, J., Riordan, L., & Shannon, D. C. (1995). Cardiac function and behavioral reactivity during infancy. *Psychophysiology, 32,* 199–207.

Spence, S. H., Donovan, C., & Brechman-Toussaint, M. (2000). The treatment of childhood social phobia: The effectiveness of a social skills training-based, cognitive-behavioural intervention, with and without parental involvement. *Journal of Child Psychology and Psychiatry and Allied Disciplines, 41,* 713–726.

Sue, S. (1977). Community mental health services to minority groups: Some optimism, some pessimism. *American Psychologist, 32,* 616–624.

Suzuki, L. A., Alexander, C. M., Lin, P.-Y., & Duffy, K. M. (2006). Psychopathology in the schools: Multicultural factors that impact assessment and intervention. *Psychology in the Schools, 43,* 429–438.

Sweeney, M., & Pine, D. (2004). Etiology of fear and anxiety. In T. H. Ollendick & J. S. March (Eds.), *Phobic and anxiety disorders in children and adolescents: A clinician's guide to effective psychosocial and pharmacological interventions* (pp. 34–60). New York: Oxford University Press.

Sze, K. M., & Wood, J. J. (in press). Cognitive behavioral treatment of comorbid anxiety disorders and social difficulties in children with high-functioning autism: A case report. *Journal of Contemporary Psychotherapy.*

Tolan, P. H., & Mitchell, M. E. (1989). Families and the therapy of antisocial and delinquent behavior. *Journal of Psychotherapy and the Family, 6,* 29–48.

Turner, W. L. (2000). Cultural considerations in family-based primary prevention programs in drug abuse. *Journal of Primary Prevention, 21,* 285–303.

U.S. Census Bureau (2001). *Overview of race and Hispanic origin. Census 2001 Brief.* Washington DC: Author.

Varjas, K., Nastasi, B. K., Moore, R. B., & Jayasena, A. (2005). Using ethnographic methods for development of culture-specific interventions. *Journal of School Psychology, 43,* 241–258.

Vasey, M. W., & Dadds, M. R. (2001). *The developmental psychopathology of anxiety.* New York: Oxford University Press.

Vernberg, E. M., & Varela, R. E. (2001). Posttraumatic stress disorder: A developmental perspective. In M. W. Vasey & M. R. Dadds (Eds.), *The developmental psychopathology of anxiety* (pp. 386–406). New York: Oxford University Press.

Warren, S. L., & Sroufe, L. A. (2004). Developmental issues. In T. H. Ollendick & J. S. March (Eds.), *Phobic and anxiety disorders in children and adolescents: A clinician's guide to effective psychosocial and pharmacological interventions* (pp. 92–115). New York: Oxford University Press.

Weiss, B., & Garber, J. (2003). Developmental differences in the phenomenology of depression. *Development and Psychopathology, 15,* 403–430.

Weisz, J. R., Jensen, A. L., & McLeod, B. D. (2005). Development and dissemination of child and adolescent psychotherapies: Milestones, methods, and a new deployment-focused model. In E. D. Hibbs & P. S. Jensen (Eds.), *Psychosocial treat-*

ments for child and adolescent disorders: Empirically-based approaches (2nd ed., pp. 9–39). Washington, DC: American Psychological Association.

Welles-Nystrom, B. (2005). Co-sleeping as a window into Swedish culture: Considerations of gender and health care. *Scandinavian Journal of Caring Sciences, 19,* 354–360.

Whitaker, A., Johnson, J., Shaffer, D., & Rapoport, J. L. (1990). Uncommon troubles in young people: Prevalence estimates of selected psychiatric disorders in a nonreferred adolescent population. *Archives of General Psychiatry, 47,* 487–496.

Wood, J. J. (2006a). Effect of anxiety reduction on children's school performance and social adjustment. *Developmental Psychology, 42,* 345–349.

Wood, J. J. (2006b). Family involvement in CBT for child anxiety disorders: Rationale, empirical support, and case study. *Psychiatric Times, 23,* 70–76.

Wood, J. J. (2006c). Parental intrusiveness and children's separation anxiety in a clinical sample. *Child Psychiatry and Human Development, 37,* 73–87.

Wood, J. J. (in press-a). Academic competence in preschool: Exploring the role of close relationships and anxiety. *Early Education and Development.*

Wood, J. J. (in press-b). Understanding and addressing attendance problems in urban schools. In G. Gates (Ed.), *Emerging thought and research on student, teacher, and administrator stress and coping.* Charlotte, NC: Information Age.

Wood, J. J., Emmerson, N. A., & Cowan, P. A. (2004). Is early attachment security carried forward into relationships with preschool peers? *British Journal of Developmental Psychology, 22,* 245–253.

Wood, J. J., McLeod, B. D., Sigman, M., Hwang, W. C., & Chu, B. C. (2003). Parenting and childhood anxiety: Theory, empirical findings, and future directions. *Journal of Child Psychology and Psychiatry and Allied Disciplines, 44,* 134–151.

REFERENCES

Wood, J. J., Piacentini, J. C., Bergman, R. L., McCracken, J., & Barrios, V. (2002). Concurrent validity of the anxiety disorders section of the Anxiety Disorders Interview Schedule for DSM-IV: Child and parent versions. *Journal of Clinical Child and Adolescent Psychology, 31,* 335–342.

Wood, J. J., Piacentini, J. C., Southam-Gerow, M., Chu, B., & Sigman, M. (2006). Family cognitive behavioral therapy for child anxiety disorders. *Journal of the American Academy of Child and Adolescent Psychiatry, 45,* 314–321.

Young, J. E. (1990). *Cognitive therapy for personality disorders: A schema-focused approach.* Sarasota, FL: Professional Resource Exchange.

Index